SPECIAL NEEDS in the early years

Physical and co-ordination difficulties

IDENTIFYING AND SUPPORTING NEEDS • ACTIVITIES COVERING EARLY LEARNING GOALS • WORKING WITH PARENTS

3/03

KU-863-082

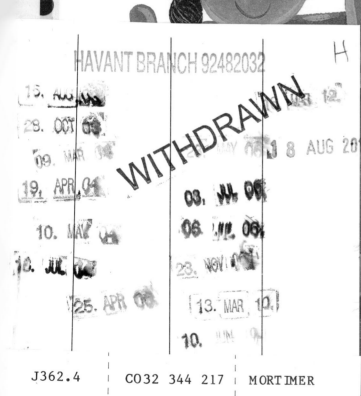

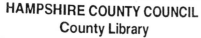

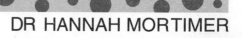
DR HANNAH MORTIMER

Author

Dr Hannah Mortimer

Editor

Jane Bishop

Assistant Editor

Saveria Mezzana

Series Designers

Sarah Rock/Anna Oliwa

Designer

Anna Oliwa

Illustrations

Shelagh McNicholas

Cover artwork

Claire Henley

Acknowledgements

The publishers gratefully acknowledge permission to reproduce the following
copyright material:
© **Gullane (Thomas) LLC 2002** for Thomas the Tank Engine & Friends
based on The Railway Series by The Rev W Awdry, on page 57.

A BRITT ALLCROFT COMPANY PRODUCTION

Qualifications and Curriculum Authority for the use of extracts from the
QCA/DfEE document *Curriculum Guidance for the Foundation Stage*
© 2000, Qualifications and Curriculum Authority.

The publishers wish to thank Makaton Vocabulary Development Project for their help in
reproducing the Makaton illustrations in this book.
Every effort has been made to trace copyright holders and the publishers apologize for any
inadvertent omissions.

Text © 2002, Hannah Mortimer
© 2002, Scholastic Ltd

Designed using Adobe Pagemaker
Published by Scholastic Ltd, Villiers House,
Clarendon Avenue, Leamington Spa, Warwickshire CV32 5PR

Visit our website at www.scholastic.co.uk

Printed by Alden Group Ltd, Oxford

1 2 3 4 5 6 7 8 9 0   2 3 4 5 6 7 8 9 0 1

British Library Cataloguing-in-Publication Data A catalogue record for this book is
available from the British Library.

ISBN 0 439 01981 8

Physical and co-ordination difficulties

CONTENTS · CONTENTS · CONTENTS · CONTENTS · CONTENTS

KNOWLEDGE AND UNDERSTANDING OF THE WORLD

PHYSICAL DEVELOPMENT

CREATIVE DEVELOPMENT

PHOTOCOPIABLES

INTRODUCTION

In every early years group there will be children with varying degrees of physical co-ordination and mobility difficulty. This book provides a range of practical ideas for including these children in the activities in your setting.

The aims of the series

There is now a new, revised *Code of Practice* for the identification and assessment of special educational needs (SEN), and early years settings will require guidance on what these changes mean to them. In addition, the QCA document *Curriculum Guidance for the Foundation Stage* emphasizes the key role that early years educators play in identifying needs and responding quickly to them. While it is generally accepted that an inclusive approach is the best one for all the children concerned, many early years practitioners feel they need guidance on what an inclusive early years curriculum might actually 'look like' in practice. The *Special Needs in the Early Years* series includes books on helping children with most kinds of special needs:

- behavioural and emotional difficulties
- speech and language difficulties
- learning difficulties
- physical and co-ordination difficulties
- autistic spectrum difficulties
- medical difficulties
- sensory difficulties.

An eighth book forms a handbook for the whole series, entitled *Special Needs Handbook* and provides general guidance and more detail on how to assess, plan for, teach and monitor children with SEN in early years settings.

Many groups will at some point include children who have physical and co-ordination difficulties. Some of these children may have significant difficulties in movement and balance and may need special walking equipment, seating or buggies. Others may be slow to develop co-ordination and clumsy in their motor control – they may have been described as having 'dyspraxic' difficulties.

This book will help all early years professionals to recognize and understand this wide range of difficulties and to provide inclusive activities for these children.

How to use this book

Chapter 1 provides an introduction to requirements under the revised *SEN Code of Practice* as it relates to children who have physical and co-ordination difficulties. There is a reminder of the requirements of the

QCA Early Learning Goals and Curriculum Guidelines across each Area of Learning. The need for individual education plans (IEPs) for children who have SEN will be introduced with information on what it means to meet SEN in an inclusive way. There are pointers for developing positive partnership and relationships with parents and families, and an introduction to some of the outside agencies with whom you may be required to liaise.

Chapter 2 looks more closely at the needs of children who have physical and co-ordination difficulties. There are ideas for trying a range of approaches and making use of the full range of resources and activities available in your setting.

Areas of Learning

There are then six activity chapters, each one related to one of the QCA Areas of Learning: Personal, social and emotional development; Communication, language and literacy; Mathematical development; Knowledge and understanding of the world; Physical development and Creative development. Each chapter contains ten activities, each with a learning objective for all the children (with or without SEN) and an individual learning target for any child who might have any one of a range of physical and co-ordination difficulties. The activities will target different kinds of difficulties in the hope that early years workers will become able to develop a flexible approach to planning inclusive activities, dipping into the ideas described in these chapters. It is

suggested that you read through the activities for their general ideas, and then select activities as and when you need them as part of your general curriculum planning.

Each activity includes advice on the optimum group size, a list of what you need, a description of what to do, any special support which might be necessary for the child with SEN, ideas for extending the activity for more able children and suggestions for links with home. These guidelines can be used flexibly depending on the needs of the children in your particular setting.

This book relates to the early years and SEN procedures followed in England, but the general guidance on individual planning, positive behaviour management and activities can be applied equally to early years provision in Scotland, Wales and Northern Ireland.

Normal physical development

Although each child is a unique and special individual, children's development appears to follow a very similar pathway. We refer to certain recognizable steps in a child's development as their 'developmental milestones'. It is helpful to spend some time looking at how developmental milestones typically progress in children's physical development. We need to make sure that children who cannot control their movements in a co-ordinated way can nevertheless gain access to

the early years curriculum. This is likely to affect our planning for them in all Areas of Learning, not just Physical development. When a child has difficulties in moving and controlling their body, we must never assume that they also have difficulties in thinking and understanding. It is important that we design new activities so that all children can participate and learn, by whatever means available to them.

The first year

During their first twelve months, most babies begin to learn to control their bodies in a purposeful and controlled way. Starting with primitive reflexes of startling, suckling and clinging, a baby will progress to making swipes and kicks which increase in frequency when the baby is

distressed or happy. In time, these movements enable the baby to knock over or to move objects, and gradually aim and timing improve. Soon, a baby learns to close a fist on fingers and proffered toys, and can shake, pick up or bang a toy for pleasure. A six-month-old baby becomes able to hold smaller objects, at first picking up all objects using a generalized scoop of the palm; in time, the forefinger begins to 'lead' as opposition of finger and thumb begins to develop.

By their first birthday, most babies are able to hold toys in each hand, bringing objects together and enjoying the feel of them as they are manipulated. Babies will delight in exploring small toys using all five senses, especially brightly-coloured objects that are easy to handle. These early explorations help them to co-ordinate their senses and understand the world around them.

Two-year-olds

Two-year-olds soon begin to develop scribbling skills, at first making feathery marks and dabs, progressing to wide scribbles. Circular scribbling emerges before the second birthday, most two-year-olds managing to copy an approximate straight line or circle. These early marks slowly develop into letter-like forms with practice. Stacking towers, throwing and pouring are all skills which develop during the second year.

Children vary enormously in the age at which they take their first steps. Some crawl first, others choose to 'bottom-shuffle' or to creep. In time, babies learn to pull themselves up against low furniture, taking their weight on their legs and bouncing up and down as they flex and stretch their muscles. At this stage, their perspective on the world changes, their whole centre of gravity moving from lying, through sitting and crawling, to standing. It is not long before they begin to stand for a moment or two without support and then take a first tentative step or two.

The first wide-legged steps develop into more fluent treads, and the waddle of the one-year-old develops into the smoother gait of the rising two-year-old. By their second birthday, most children are climbing or walking up and down stairs, seating themselves at a table, running, jumping and beginning to balance.

Aged three and over

Three-year-olds perfect these skills: they can balance on one leg for a few moments, run and change direction, and most are beginning to pedal a wheeled toy. They can also walk upstairs one foot on each step, run and change directions as they go, and are beginning to throw and kick a ball with aim.

If this pattern of development is delayed or interrupted in some way, because a child has difficulty in making or co-ordinating movements, there is a risk that their whole learning will be affected. If a child cannot move towards items of interest to them or take part in the range of actions that children usually perform to find out about objects and toys, then their opportunities for exploration and learning will be limited.

Early years educators need to understand the difficulties of a child who has SEN in detail and to plan ways of making sure that each child has access to early learning or, as a last resort, to bring the early learning to them. In the next chapter, we look at the implications of this for your setting.

Using a wide range of resources

The activities encourage the use of a wide range of resources and materials available in early years settings. There are ideas for art and craft, story time and physical play, and for exploring and finding out. Special use is made of circle-time approaches as they have been shown to be very effective in building children's self-esteem and confidence, and in teaching them how to demonstrate new skills within a group. Using a regular music circle time can enhance looking, listening, joining in and confidence within circle time and beyond, and many of the activities use a musical approach too. Young children who are reluctant to receive individual physiotherapy may still enjoy doing the same exercises to music as part of a group action game.

Links with home

All the activities suggest ways of keeping closely in touch with the children's homes. By sharing activities with parents and carers, you can also play a role in helping the carers of a child who has physical and co-ordination difficulties to follow approaches which will offer encouragement at home.

Providing special support

You need to make sure that any child with SEN in your group is accessing the full range of your early years provision. Clearly this cannot happen if the child is isolated in any way or withdrawn from the group regularly, and this is another reason for collecting ideas for inclusive group activities. 'Support' does not have to mean individual one-to-one attention. Instead, it can mean playing alongside a child or watching so as to encourage new learning, staying 'one step ahead' of any problem times (such as when the children are moving around quickly or enjoying outdoor play), and sometimes teaching the child in small groups. You will find suggestions for doing this in Chapter 2.

THE LEGAL REQUIREMENTS

This chapter explains your legal requirements towards children with physical and co-ordination difficulties. There are ideas for planning and monitoring their progress and for working with parents and carers as well as other professionals.

The *Code of Practice* for SEN

The *SEN Code of Practice* is a guide for school governors, registered early years providers and local education authorities (LEAs) about the practical help that they can give to children with special educational needs. It recommends that schools and early years providers should identify children's needs and take action to meet those needs as early as possible, working with parents and carers. The aim is to enable all pupils

with SEN to reach their full potential, to be included fully in their school communities and make a successful transition to adulthood. The Code gives guidance to schools and early years providers, but it does not tell them what they must do in every case.

In 1996, the DfEE stated that all pre-school providers in the voluntary and non-maintained sectors who registered to redeem vouchers should also have regard to the *Code of Practice*. This continues to be the case for groups registering with the Local Education Authority under the Early Years Development and Childcare Partnerships.

There is now a revised *SEN Code of Practice* and this is described more fully in the handbook accompanying this series, *Special Needs Handbook* by Hannah Mortimer.

The *Code of Practice* principles

The underlying principles for early years settings are that all children have a right to a broad and balanced curriculum which enables them to make maximum progress towards the Early Learning Goals. Early years practitioners must recognize, identify and meet SEN within their settings. Most children with SEN will be in a local mainstream early years group, even those who have 'statements of SEN'. Parents, carers, children, early years settings, and support services should work as partners in planning for and meeting SEN.

The *Code of Practice* is designed to enable practitioners to identify and address SEN early. These SEN will normally be met in the local mainstream setting, though some children may need extra consideration or help to be able to fully access the early years curriculum.

Early Years Action Plus

Good practice can take many forms, and early years providers are encouraged to adopt a flexible and a graduated response to the SEN of individual children. This approach recognizes that there is a continuum of SEN and, where necessary, brings increasing specialist expertise on board if the child is experiencing continuing difficulties.

Once a child's SEN have been identified, the providers should intervene through 'Early Years Action'. This intervention is co-ordinated by one person within the setting who has been designated as the Special Educational Needs Co-ordinator (SENCO), with other adults sharing the responsibility of supporting the child.

When reviewing the child's progress and the help that they are receiving, the provider might decide to seek alternative approaches to learning through the advice of the outside support services. These interventions are known as 'Early Years Action Plus', which is characterized by the involvement of specialists from outside the setting. The SENCO continues to take a leading role, working closely with the member of staff responsible for the child, and:

● draws on the advice from outside specialists such as early years support teachers or educational psychologists;
● ensures that the child and their parents or carers are consulted and kept informed;
● ensures that an IEP is drawn up, incorporating the specialist advice, and that it is included in the curriculum planning for the whole setting;
● with outside specialists, monitors and reviews the child's progress;
● keeps the Head of the setting informed.

Statements of SEN

For a very few children, the help provided by Early Years Action Plus will still not be sufficient to ensure satisfactory progress. The provider, external professional and parents or carers may then decide to ask the LEA to consider carrying out a statutory assessment of the child's SEN.

The LEA must decide quickly whether or not it has the 'evidence' to indicate that a statutory assessment is necessary for a child. It is then responsible for co-ordinating a statutory assessment and will call for the various reports that it requires, from the early years teacher (usually a support teacher, early years practitioner or LEA nursery teacher), an educational psychologist, a doctor (who will also gather 'evidence' from any therapists involved), and the Social Services Department if involved, and will ask the parents or carers to submit their own views and evidence. Once it has collected in the evidence, the LEA might decide to issue a 'statement of SEN' for the child. Only children with severe and long-standing SEN go on to receive a statement (about two per cent of all children). There are various rights of appeal in the cases of disagreement, and each LEA can provide information about these.

Requirements of the Early Learning Goals

Registered early years providers are required to deliver a broad and balanced curriculum across the six Areas of Learning as defined in the *Curriculum Guidance for the Foundation Stage* (QCA). This paves the way for children's early learning to be followed through into Baseline Assessment measures on entry to school and into National Curriculum

assessment for school-age children. The integration of these three areas should contribute to the earlier identification of children who are experiencing difficulties in making progress.

The Early Learning Goals prescribed by the QCA have been set into context so that they are seen as an aid to planning rather than as an early years curriculum. Practical examples of Stepping Stones towards the Goals are provided in the QCA document. Within this book, each activity is linked to a learning objective for *all* the group, and also to an *individual* learning target for any child who has physical and co-ordination difficulties.

OFSTED

Defining a set of Early Learning Goals that most children will have attained by the end of their Foundation Stage (the end of their Reception year) has helped to ensure that nursery education is of good quality and provides a sound preparation for later schooling. To ensure that nursery education is of good quality, early years providers registered with their local Early Years Development and Childcare Partnership are required to have their educational provision inspected regularly. The nursery inspectors, appointed by the Office for Standards in Education (OFSTED) assess the quality of the early years educational provision, look at the clarity of roles and responsibilities within the setting, and are interested in plans for meeting the needs of individual children (including those with SEN) and for developing improved partnership with parents and carers.

The need for individual education plans

One characteristic of Early Years Action for a child with SEN is the writing of the individual education plan. This is a detailed plan which aims to ensure that a child will make progress. An example of an IEP is shown on the next page.

IEPs should be reviewed regularly with the parents or carers and should be seen as an integrated aspect of the curriculum planning for the whole group. They should only include details which are additional to or different from the differentiated early years curriculum that is in place for all the children in the group.

Case study: Richard

Richard is four. He is an alert little boy who takes a lively interest in his surroundings and loves to play and to explore. When he was a baby, it was noticed that his muscles were rather floppy and poorly controlled. He was slow to crawl and to balance, and also found it difficult to pick up or to release small toys. He has learned to talk and enjoys communicating with adults and with other children, but still tends to speak rather unclearly. He also seems to be unsure of exactly where his body is in space. All these difficulties are related to his condition of mild cerebral palsy. His pre-school teachers are monitoring his needs through

Individual education plan

Name: Richard	**Early Years Action Plus**

Nature of difficulty: Richard has some physical disabilities related to his mild cerebral palsy. He walks unsteadily, speaks rather unclearly and finds it hard to control his fine finger movements.

Action

1 Seeking training
Richard needs to adopt the correct postures when sitting and standing. We will ask the physiotherapist to visit us to show us how to encourage these and what we should do to encourage Richard's motor development.

2 Creating the right environment
We will make sure that everyone keeps the floors and play areas clear from obstacles. We will closely supervise the children when they are playing on the cars and bikes so that Richard does not get knocked or lose confidence. We will also make sure that all the helpers know how to position Richard when he is standing or sitting to play.

3 Planning the curriculum
● We will ask the early years support teacher for ideas for encouraging Richard's play skills and hand movements.
● We will borrow specialist toys from the Toy Library at the Community Centre.
● Richard's mother has agreed to bring in the homework book that Richard's speech and language therapist uses when he sees him every month. We will also use these ideas in the group.
● The occupational therapist will let us have ideas for developing Richard's two-handed play and pincer grasp.

Help from parents
Richard's mother will bring in his special walker for us to use in the group, and make sure that the therapy diary is up to date and is shared between us all. She will also tell us which cup and squeezy scissors to buy.

Targets for this term
● Richard will roll a ball to another child using two hands. This will be done by his helper playing alongside him and supporting his hands as he pushes and receives the ball. We will keep the activity fun so that Richard is encouraged to try on his own.
● Richard will walk more confidently around the playroom with his rollator walker, avoiding obstacles successfully. We will encourage him to concentrate on looking where he is going.
● Richard will be able to speak clearly in short phrases and make himself understood. This will be achieved by our repeating back to Richard what he has said so that he hears the words clearly.
● Richard will be able to connect the rail tracks on the train set and build a small tower of five bricks. We will first teach him on a one-to-one basis and then help him to generalize these skills into his free play.
● Richard will be able to copy a straight line with a chubby crayon and to snip with his squeezable scissors. We will use craft and model sessions to make this fun.

Review meeting with parents: Next term. Invite the occupational therapist, physiotherapist and early years support teacher.

Early Years Action Plus under the *SEN Code of Practice*, with outside advice from the early years support teacher and the physiotherapist. They must therefore draw up an individual education plan at least every term, and meet with the parents or carers and outside professionals regularly to review it. You will find a blank pro forma on page 85.

Working with parents and carers

The parents or carers of children with SEN often ask how they can help at home when areas of concern are expressed by the early years setting. They might also approach staff with their own concerns. Parents are the primary educators of their children and should be included as an essential part of the whole-group approach to meeting a child's needs from the start. They have expert knowledge on their own child, and it is important to create an ethos which shows how much this information is valued and made use of. Information-sharing is important and is a two-way process.

To involve the parents in meeting their child's needs:

● Make a personal invitation to parents and carers, who may not always call in to the setting on a daily basis. Invite them in to share information about their children's achievements, and draw their attention to a specific display, for example, where samples of their children's work can be seen.

● Show the carers what their child has already achieved and improvements in their skills that have been made within the setting. Do not make them feel too despondent if there have not been improvements at home. Use the 'good news' as a hope for positive changes to come.

● Ask the child to show their parents what they can do, what they can say, or what they have learned.

● Ask the carers for their opinions by allowing opportunities for them to contribute information and share experiences. It is often helpful to set a regular time aside when other demands will not intrude.

● Thank the parents regularly for their support.

● Celebrate success with the carers to ensure an ongoing positive partnership.

● Use a home–setting diary to keep in touch and to provide a two-way system of sharing information about a child's success, experiences and opportunities.

Working with outside agencies

When assessing and working with a young child who has SEN, an outside professional may be involved in helping an early years group to monitor and meet the child's needs. For children with physical and co-ordination difficulties, this is likely to be an early years support teacher, a physiotherapist, an occupational therapist or members of the local Child Development Team. The kinds of advice and support available will vary with local policies and practices.

Physiotherapists

Following assessment and therapeutic diagnosis, they will work closely with the parents or carers to establish appropriate goals for the child. This individually-planned programme might cover careful positioning and movement, advice and support, special handling skills, exercise regimes, walking practice, balance and co-ordination exercises, stretching of muscles, chest physiotherapy and special equipment.

Most paediatric physiotherapists are involved in the assessment of gross motor skills and treatment of motor delay. They work particularly with children who have physical disabilities and delay, giving advice on handling and care, lifting, positioning, nasal suctioning, inhibiting abnormal reflexes, and on splints, boots, braces, wheelchairs and buggies, sometimes with overlap with the occupational therapist. They contribute to team assessments by advising on goals and interventions for motor skills, and often particularly liaise with the hospital services. Sometimes, advice is given on the use of therapeutic electrical equipment.

Physiotherapists provide stretching and direct physiotherapy and pass these ideas to the carers to follow at home. Some physiotherapists also work to help carers relax and avoid the physiological effects of stress.

Occupational therapists

They can work with children whose development is interrupted by physical, psychological or social impairment or disability. They aim to develop the child's maximum level of independence by improving practical life skills, to promote a better quality of life. They work in conjunction with the child's family in a variety of settings and assess gross and fine motor skills, any dyspraxic difficulties, writing skills, independence skills, visual perception and body awareness, and the need for specialized equipment for home and the setting, including seating, wheelchairs, toilet and bathing aids, and adaptive equipment to improve everyday skills. Sometimes they provide a specialist assessment of switches and information technology. They are also called upon to advise on handedness for a child beginning to write where this is still undetermined.

A Portage home visitor

They are sometimes involved in helping a child to learn new steps in their development. It is helpful to meet with the parents or carers and a Portage worker so that you can learn about the approaches which have been helpful to the child (see any Portage Assessment checklist [NFER-Nelson]) and use this as a starting-point for your own teaching and monitoring.

Sometimes it is you who will be identifying a child's learning difficulties for the first time. You might reach the stage where you feel that outside professional help is needed. Usually a request for help from outside agencies is likely to follow a decision taken by the SENCO, colleagues and parents when reviewing a child's progress in the setting.

HELPING CHILDREN WITH PHYSICAL AND CO-ORDINATION DIFFICULTIES

This chapter explores why children might have 'physical difficulties', either because development is slow or due to a medical condition, and suggests how to include them in an early years curriculum.

The conditions covered

Within the term 'physical and co-ordination difficulties' comes a wide range of needs. There are children with mobility difficulties who have not yet learned to walk – they may be creeping, moving with a rollator, or a few may be in buggies or (rarely at this age) wheelchairs. Sometimes this will be because of a recognized condition such as cerebral palsy or spina bifida. Sometimes it will be because their physical development is delayed for their age because of general learning difficulties or other causes. There are also children with fine-motor problems who find it hard to dress, to hold a pencil or to make small finger movements. A few of these children may have been described as 'dyspraxic' and hand in hand with this condition come clumsiness and problems with perception, language, body awareness and sometimes with memory and organization.

This chapter explains some of these conditions, their prevalence and causes, and how you might support any children affected in your early years setting.

Children who have mobility difficulties

The physical development of some children might be at an earlier stage than their peers. Perhaps they have not yet learned to walk, although they can move around by crawling, creeping or rolling. Most of these children will learn to walk in time, though a very few may never walk and move independently because of their condition. These children may continue to be dependent on other people and on special equipment for moving around.

Mobility difficulties might be caused by a named condition. Children with cerebral palsy (see page 17) may have a part of their brain which is not working properly or not developing normally. Children with spina bifida (see pages 18 and 19) are born with a fault in their spinal column. Children with named conditions such as these will still present a wide range of abilities and needs: some will make good progress towards walking, while others will always need considerable help, depending on the parts of their brains or bodies affected. In other cases, a child might be delayed in moving and balancing because their whole development is progressing more gradually than for other children of the same age. These children can be helped to learn movement and balance skills step by small step.

Some children may be given special equipment to help them sit, stand, move and balance. They may have a special buggy or

wheelchair, may use a rollator or standing frame, or have special chairs or wedges for seating or for lying. Other children may need orthopaedic boots or splints to support weak muscles and to make them more steady. Most children with mobility difficulties will already be known to the physiotherapist and/or the occupational therapist.

Supporting children with mobility difficulties

Consider the provision you have from the point of view of a child with mobility difficulties:

● Are your floor surfaces clean and welcoming?
● Are they comfortable to crawl or roll on?
● Are there areas for running and wheeled toys, and other areas safe for floor play?
● Are your toys and equipment accessible for a child with mobility difficulties?
● Could a child with mobility difficulties still make choices and play independently?
● Are your spaces accessible to children in wheelchairs or with rollators?
● Could the children open doors, reach for equipment, play at the same physical level as the other children?

Find out if there is any special equipment you might need to provide.

Contact the physiotherapist or occupational therapist for advice on seating and positioning, and use the child's parents as the 'experts' who will keep you in touch with how to use the equipment. Know also when to stand back and allow the child to be independent. Look for wheeled toys with a firm base which can be pushed or scooted along from a lying or sitting position. The occupational therapy service should be able to advise you.

Provide opportunities for playing together in different positions (lying, kneeling, sitting or standing at a table) and use the suggestions within the activities in this book. Look for opportunities to encourage larger movement and balance in a safe way, such as the use of soft play equipment, ball pools and inflatable toys. Ensure that your picture books and stories reflect a wide range of abilities, including children who have wheelchairs. You will find some ideas for specialist book companies on page 95.

Children who have cerebral palsy

The term 'cerebral palsy' is widely used and can cover mild clumsiness right through to a severe physical disability affecting both arms and legs. No two children with cerebral palsy will be alike, and it is

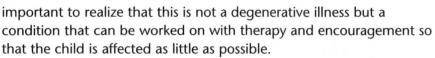

important to realize that this is not a degenerative illness but a condition that can be worked on with therapy and encouragement so that the child is affected as little as possible.

About 1,500 babies are born with or develop cerebral palsy every year in Britain. It is caused when part of the child's brain is not working properly so that body movements cannot be controlled by the muscles. Sometimes this brain injury is caused by an early infection during pregnancy, sometimes by a bleed in the brain in very premature babies, sometimes by a loss of oxygen to the brain, or sometimes because the brain has not developed normally. The effect of this is that the messages from brain to muscles and back again become jumbled.

There are three main forms of cerebral palsy which you may hear described if you have a child with this condition in your group.

● In 'spastic cerebral palsy', the child's movements look stiff and they find it very hard to control some or all of their muscles. Perhaps only one side of the body is affected, in which case the child is described as having 'hemiplegia'. In 'diplegia', only the legs are affected, or perhaps the arms are only mildly affected and in 'quadriplegia' both arms and legs will be affected.

● In 'athetoid cerebral palsy', a child's muscles might change rapidly from floppy to tense, with the result that they are in constant uncontrolled movement. Their speech may be unclear too, since the tongue and voice will be difficult to control.

● In 'ataxic cerebral palsy', children find it extremely difficult to balance, and those who learn to walk may continue to be very unsteady on their feet.

Many children have a combination of two or more types of cerebral palsy, so it becomes difficult to say which type is causing them the most difficulties.

The symptoms of cerebral palsy might be very slight, or so severe that the child needs help in every day-to-day task. Their movements may be slow and awkward, floppy or stiff, poorly controlled, and sometimes unwanted – for example, sometimes when a child particularly wants to reach for a toy, a muscle spasm might cause his arm to move backwards, just at the time he wants to reach it forwards. The more excited he becomes and the more he tries, the more his movements might work against him. Some children develop whole patterns of unwanted movement which the physiotherapist can help you to recognize and work with, by using the correct seating and positioning, and keeping arousal as calm as possible.

You must never assume that because children have considerable physical difficulties they will also be slow in their thinking and intelligence. Clearly, these children will not have had the same early learning experiences as children without a physical difficulty, so here is where your setting can begin to redress the balance. Sometimes specialist

equipment such as the right computer and artificial voice systems is needed. Only when all the opportunities to learn have been presented can you assume that a child also has significant learning difficulties.

Supporting children with cerebral palsy

There is no cure for cerebral palsy, but symptoms can be worked on and improved for a child at an early stage. Seating, posture and positioning are vitally important to prevent problems in bones later on. You will need to talk to the parents or carers about the correct ways to physically handle their child, and hopefully meet with the physiotherapist and occupational therapist. It should be possible for you to borrow the correct table, chair or buggy from the hospital, Social Services or through the parents. The therapists will also be able to show you how to play with the child in a way that makes the best use of their movements. Find out just what you need to do to cope with nappies or toilet routines, feeding and drinking, and how much help is needed with dressing and undressing.

Once you know how to help on the physical side, consider how you can help the child to experience all the hands-on play activities that the other children in your group are enjoying. Think of the different play areas in turn and consider how you can help this child to fully explore the sand tray, the water tray and the painting and sticking table. Can the child begin to play with shapes and different materials, to enjoy stories and music, to talk and to listen in the group? As an early years specialist, you will need to draw on your creativity to work out how the child can make the best of your provision despite any physical difficulties.

Children with spina bifida and hydrocephalus

These two conditions are present from birth and affect children's physical and neurological development. Most babies born with spina bifida also have hydrocephalus.

Spina bifida is a congenital defect in the spinal cord, where one of the vertebrae (or bones which form the backbone) has failed to form properly, leaving a gap or split. It happens very early in pregnancy and the spinal cord may not develop properly, forming a cyst or protrusion outside the spine. The amount of disability resulting from this defect depends on how greatly the spinal cord is affected, where the bifida is and the amount of nerve damage involved.

Often there is paralysis below the split, with incontinence and a difficulty in or incapability of walking. Spina bifida causes a physical disability and it is only in some cases that the child may also have learning difficulties. There is a higher risk of having a baby with spina bifida if the condition already occurs in the family, and genetic counselling is usually available for these families.

Hydrocephalus is a condition in which the cerebro-spinal fluid accumulates in the brain, causing a swelling of the ventricles of the brain – the fluid cannot drain freely. Because their skull is still soft, a baby with hydrocephalus might develop an enlarged head, and some children will need a shunting device to be inserted in their brain by operation to allow the fluid to drain. This needs careful monitoring to ensure that it works effectively and that no infection develops.

Some forms of hydrocephalus need no treatment and settle down in time. Health visitors are careful to monitor the baby's head circumference in the early stages.

Supporting children with spina bifida and hydrocephalus

Talk to the parents or carers about what the condition means for their particular child. Establish how much support is needed to help the child move around, reach, join in and stay clean and dry. If the child uses a buggy, special seating or standing frames, ask the parents to show you

how to use them so that you can make any adjustments necessary during the session. Allow the carers to show you any changing routines for the first session or two so that you quickly become confident in taking over from them. This will be reassuring for both of you. Check if there is anything that you need to know about risk of infection.

Find out about a child's strengths and interests so that you can allow the child to play independently whenever possible, encouraging them to let you know when they need your help. Aim to be available and responsive to this.

Make sure that your tables and easels are at the right height for any special seats or buggies, and try to store your craft activities and toys at a level that allows all the children to make choices and reach for them. If you find that the child is missing out on an activity because of being in the wrong position, contact the occupational therapist for ideas on how to improve this.

Look for opportunities to fully involve the child in all physical activities, including outdoor trips, movement and dance (complete with buggy and colourful chiffon scarves to wave), music sessions with instruments and carpet games. In particular, any toys which encourage looking, listening, careful handling, language and imagination will be ideal.

Sometimes you might find that special adaptations are needed for your premises to help with changing or mobility. This is not so likely with little children, but if you are worried about your physical environment, ask the parents or occupational therapist whether changes are needed or whether there is equipment available that would make the session easier to manage. Remember to use these early contacts with the family sensitively and to inspire their confidence.

Children with dyspraxia

Some children appear to be clumsy in their movements. They find it hard to learn how to move and balance smoothly. They may also be poor in organizing themselves and find it difficult to speak clearly and to understand where their bodies are in space. Compared to other children of their age, these children may find it hard to dress and undress, have a poor pencil grip, find jigsaws and puzzles difficult to do and have poor balance when they are running or climbing. They may or may not have been diagnosed as 'dyspraxic'. You will need to identify any difficulties in co-ordination and take steps to help the child improve their skills.

There is usually no particular cause or neurological impairment, and it is thought that dyspraxia is related to an immaturity in the brain rather than to any damage. It can therefore usually be improved with practice, with maturity and with exercises.

Some children with dyspraxia are helped by occupational therapists who provide exercises to improve co-ordination. Other children might see speech and language therapists who help them to co-ordinate their mouth and tongue movements and learn to speak more clearly.

Supporting children with dyspraxia

Keep motor activities as fun and motivating as possible. Children with dyspraxia will need lots of practice but will soon 'opt out' if the activities are repetitive and beyond their ability. If a child speaks unclearly, repeat their words back to them more clearly to check that you have

understood and to provide a model. Keep activities short and end on a successful and positive note.

Provide large materials for fine motor tasks (such as threading cotton reels onto thick pipe-cleaners or stacking large parcels) and progress to smaller materials as the child's skills improve (such as threading centimetre beads onto bootlaces or stacking small cubes). Much of the 'special support' suggested in the activity chapters relates to providing larger materials or breaking steps down to make them more manageable for the child. Look for motivating ways of encouraging the child to have 'clever fingers', such as musical keyboards and computer activities.

Make sure that the chair is the right height for the child's feet to be firmly on the floor when sitting at a table. Try to keep distractions to a minimum when doing an activity which requires good co-ordination, perhaps by withdrawing to a quieter space or having a smaller group of children.

Encourage good eye contact when communicating. It is important to develop other 'looking skills' too: use large balls to encourage looking, tracking and catching. Try picture symbols to encourage the child to understand what happens next in the daily routine and to help them organize themselves.

Music time is useful for encouraging finger and hand actions. Many percussion instruments are fun to use, yet involve clever finger and hand movements. Use circle time to encourage remembering and guessing, building the child's self-esteem in any ways you can.

Case study: Jake
This case study gives an illustration of how to support a child.

Jake is four years old and has been diagnosed as having 'dyspraxic' difficulties.

Introducing Jake
Jake was four when his parents were told he was dyspraxic. They had always felt that Jake's development was different from their other two children. He seemed very active as a baby and was rarely still. However, he learned to move around rather late, preferring a 'bottom-shuffle' to a crawl and tumbling a lot when he sat. He took a long time to pick small toys up, tending to use a full palmar grasp and a grab. As a toddler, he was not at all interested in learning to dress himself, and there were frequent temper tantrums if his parents insisted.

Jake was a very messy eater and continued to fall over a lot and bump into objects. He showed no interest in construction bricks and, although he learned to use crayons, he held them in a very tight, grabbing movement, quickly tiring and losing interest.

About this time, Jake's language seemed to be slow to develop and his initial referral for help was through the health visitor, who noticed this delay at his two-year check, to the local speech and language therapist. Jake still sees the therapist for help with his speech, but he was also assessed by the occupational therapist because his difficulties were felt to be wider than language alone.

In children with dyspraxia, it seems that messages to the brain to do with movement, balance and co-ordination take longer, or do not flow smoothly. Practising movements and speech sounds which reinforce these nerve networks can actually help dyspraxic children to improve their skills.

How to help

The occupational therapist suggested three ways of helping. She encouraged Jake's mother to take him along to a 'Tumble Tots' group where he could enjoy practising movement and balance with other children (contact details on page 95). She also set Jake some daily exercises in balancing, moving and ball play. She was keen to see Jake improve his large arm movements before he learned to refine these into smaller and finer movements, which would enable him to control a pencil later. Finally, she suggested that Jake could be helped at his local early years group.

Going to nursery

Jake was already due to start at his local nursery and was looking forward to it. The occupational therapist visited the group and explained what Jake's needs were and how the staff could help. Jake found it hard to settle in at first, flitting from activity to activity and not being able to sit still at drinks time or for a story. One of the adults played alongside Jake to provide the encouragement he needed to gradually build up his concentration. She also made sure that Jake knew what was expected of him, showing him how to do things first, or helping him to hold a crayon in the right position. He was helped to sit squarely on a chair with his feet firmly on the ground, and given a cushion to mark his place when sitting on the floor.

Jake loved the sand and water trays and was shown how to make patterns with his fingers. He was encouraged to develop his sense of touch with feely-bag games and collage pictures using different textures and shapes. He soon moved onto play dough and clay, poking, rolling, shaping and cutting it up. This was an easy way for Jake to develop his fine finger movements, without feeling pressured. He used special scissors, recommended by

his therapist, to encourage cutting, and gradually moved from chubby finger crayons to finer tools. As he begun to feel more successful in front of the other children, he begun to practise throwing and catching with huge sponge balls and beanbags. Jake's language also began to become clearer as he enjoyed more interaction with the other children.

Developing inclusive practice

'Inclusion' is the practice of including all children together in a setting so that all the children participate fully in the regular routines and group activities, even though these might need to be modified to meet individual children's goals and objectives. The activities in this book carry learning objectives for all the children (with and without SEN) and individual targets for the child who has physical and co-ordination difficulties.

There seem to be certain common features that promote inclusion:

● Careful joint planning. For example, if there is special support for a child, how will it be used? Will the child still have access to the full range of adults, children and activities?

● Staff use of educational labels rather than categories or medical labels, such as 'mobility difficulty' rather than 'spastic', 'co-ordination difficulty' rather than 'dyspraxic', or even 'child who has SEN' rather than 'SEN child'.

● Teachers and adults provide good role models for the children because of their positive expectations and the way they respect and value the children.

● Special attention is given to improving children's access and communication skills.

● Teaching strategies are developed which enable all children to participate and to learn.

● Individual approaches are planned which draw on children's earlier experiences, set high expectations and encourage mutual peer support.

● There is a flexible use of support aimed at promoting joining in and inclusion rather than at creating barriers and exclusion.

How inclusive is your policy?

● Do you make it clear that your setting is inclusive and that it welcomes all children, whatever their individual needs?

● Is this clearly stated in any parents' handbooks?

- Does your setting meet the requirements of the *SEN Code of Practice*?
- Do staff members have the opportunities to take up training in both special needs and early years practice?
- Is your curriculum planning suitable for all children? Are there opportunities for all children to have positive outcomes from each learning opportunity that you plan?
- Do you share observations and planning with parents and carers on a regular basis?
- Do you use methods of communication that include everyone, and that can be used between children (such as including sign language and using more than one language within the setting)?
- Are you prepared to be flexible and change what you are doing in order to meet a particular child's needs?
- Are you happy to involve professionals from outside agencies and to include them in your planning?
- Will all your staff work and plan together to meet any special educational needs?
- Can you provide families with the names and contact details of relevant support services?

Trying a range of approaches

In an inclusive approach, children with SEN are defined not in terms of their condition or label but in terms of the difficulties that they are experiencing (and their particular strengths too). So what you will be observing is not a condition, a syndrome or certain signs, but the fact that a particular child is not making the progress that you might hope for in your setting, given their age and the fact that they have had time to settle with you.

Your task is to make your early years provision accessible to all children, regardless of their disabilities. The two main ways in which you can set out to achieve this is by making sure that the curriculum you offer is both inclusive (for everybody) and differentiated (to the needs of the child with SEN). The ideas in the activity chapters of this book provide opportunities for all children, with special support for any child who has physical and co-ordination difficulties. As no two children's needs are the same, even if they have been diagnosed as having the same condition you will need to read through all the activities, picking and choosing the ideas as they apply to your situation, and developing your own ideas for support in a flexible way.

PERSONAL, SOCIAL AND EMOTIONAL DEVELOPMENT

These activities will help the children to develop in confidence, join in with group activities, be more independent and begin to think about other people's feelings and needs.

Meet Ted

Group size
Six to 15 children.

What you need
A large teddy bear or other soft toy.

What to do
Sit down together for circle time. To include all the children, try and ensure that you are all sitting at the same height. So, if one of the children must sit in special seating or in a wheelchair or buggy, arrange for all the children to sit in chairs. If the physiotherapist has recommended that circle time be used for a child with motor problems to practise lying on a wedge, then arrange for all the children to sit on cushions or shapes. Look for ways of making all the children feel included and part of your group.

Introduce Teddy to the group, wave his paw and pretend to let him whisper in your ear. Tell the children that he would like to meet them all. When Teddy whispers to you once more, explain to the children that he does not know their names and ask them to introduce Teddy to their friends.

Turn to the child next to you and say, 'Teddy, this is (Ali)'. Pass Teddy to Ali and encourage Ali to make a fuss of him and make him feel welcome. Support the children as they pass Teddy around the circle, introducing him by name to their neighbours.

When Teddy returns to you, let him whisper in your ear again and tell the children that Teddy says 'thank you' for making him feel so welcome.

Special support
If a child has difficulties in grasping Teddy, support them gently so that they can hold their arms around him. If speech is a problem, encourage a sign to Teddy (a brief wave perhaps) and help the child to say the introduction, prompting the first letter sound for their neighbour's name, 'Teddy, this is A...'. Allow time for their response; it can take children with co-ordination difficulties longer than usual to process and carry out actions.

Extension
Allow the children to choose who to introduce Teddy to in the circle, carrying him to a friend and introducing him. Make sure that every child has a turn.

LEARNING OBJECTIVE FOR ALL THE CHILDREN
● to be confident to speak in a familiar group.

INDIVIDUAL LEARNING TARGETS
● to say their name
● to raise their heads to give eye contact when greeted.

LINKS WITH HOME
Encourage the children to introduce Teddy to their parents or carers at home time. Teddy Bear introductions are a lovely way of getting to know one another and your families!

LEARNING OBJECTIVE FOR ALL THE CHILDREN
● to develop personal independence.

INDIVIDUAL LEARNING TARGETS
● to use a fork to stab food
● to develop a simple aim.

Hungry clown

Group size
Three or four children.

What you need
The photocopiable sheet on page 86; A3 and A4 paper and card; washable chubby felt-tipped pens; glue and brushes; sticky shapes; child-safe scissors; play dough; pastry boards; cutters; rollers; strong plastic plates; plastic knives, forks and spoons; empty cereal boxes.

What to do
Split this activity in two parts, perhaps on consecutive sessions. Copy the photocopiable sheet picturing a clown's head on to A3 or A4 paper (A3 paper will be best if there are children with co-ordination difficulties). Give each child a sheet to colour in and stick shapes on to. Encourage the children to make their clowns brightly coloured and funny. Now help the children to paste the backs of their clowns with glue and mount them on to card. Place them on one side to dry. When the clowns are dry, help the children to cut them out, then cut out the mouth shape for each child. Stick the clown's head on to the side of a cereal box (as shown in the diagram, see left) to form a 'hungry clown'.

In the second session, set out the play dough and pastry equipment for the children. Enjoy shaping and rolling the play dough together as you make 'food' for the clown.

Arrange the clown's dinner on a plate and then support the children as they use the spoons and forks, or knives and forks, to pop the food into his mouth.

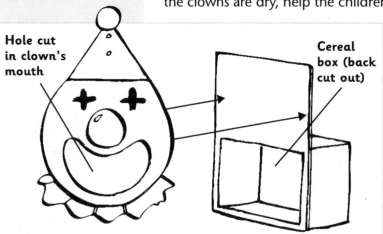

Hole cut in clown's mouth

Cereal box (back cut out)

Special support
Make use of any special sciss[or] spoons that might have beer recommended by the occup[ational] therapist. There are details of on page 96. Let children who co-ordination difficulties star[t] popping the food in with fin[ger] using a fork to stab the food. gentle hand-over-hand supp[ort] assist their aim.

Extension
Use the clown posting boxes for a letter-posting or a sorting game.

LINKS WITH HOME
Use this activity to support the work that parents and carers might be doing at home to encourage their children to feed themselves or to use a knife and fork.

Socks box

Group size
Two to six children.

What you need
Several pairs of large, brightly-coloured socks; large decorated box; carpeted area.

What to do
Place the sock collection in the box and gather together on the carpet. Introduce the socks box and encourage the children to enjoy rummaging and searching for pairs together. Invite the children to take off their shoes and to pull the socks on, over their own socks. Sit in a circle with your feet together enjoying the patterns and colours that you are making.

Now take off the large socks and put them back in the box. Take away some of the socks so that there is just one pair for each child and no more inside the box. Take it in turns to bring out one sock and put it on. Repeat so that each child has two socks, but not matching ones. Again, sit in your circle and this time see if you can take it in turns to touch foot to foot with the person who is wearing your matching sock! Use this activity as an opportunity for practising taking shoes and socks off and putting them on again.

Special support
Teach a child who has co-ordination difficulties to remove their socks by pulling them down to the heel and asking the child to pull them off the toes. Gradually extend this by encouraging the child to pull the sock off from higher up their foot or leg. This kind of step-by-step teaching is called 'backward chaining' and can be applied to other dressing and undressing skills.

Extension
Play a 'Pairs' game with playing cards, in which the children turn over two cards and must try to remember where the matching pairs are.

LEARNING OBJECTIVES FOR ALL THE CHILDREN
● to match and talk about simple patterns
● to dress and undress independently.

INDIVIDUAL LEARNING TARGET
● to pull off a sock.

LINKS WITH HOME
Share progress on dressing and undressing skills so that you are teaching these independence skills both at home and in the setting.

PERSONAL, SOCIAL & EMOTIONAL DEVELOPMENT

LEARNING OBJECTIVES FOR ALL THE CHILDREN
● to understand that there needs to be agreed codes of polite behaviour for groups of people
● to use conventions such as greetings, 'please' and 'thank you'.

INDIVIDUAL LEARNING TARGET
● to use the Makaton signs for 'please' and 'thank you'.

LINKS WITH HOME
Tell parents and carers that you have been working on saying 'please' and 'thank you' in your group and ask them to encourage these words at home as well. If a child does not say the words automatically, the carers could supply them so that the child always comes to hear the words even though they are not yet saying the words themselves.

May I help you?

Group size
Three or four children at a time.

What you need
Wheeled and pedal toys in a large hall or outdoor play area; carton boxes; plastic piping; chalk or removable coloured plastic tape.

What to do
Encourage the children to enjoy a driving game in the wheeled vehicles and pedal toys. Involve yourself in order to help the children develop the game with more imagination. Ask them if they would like a road or a roundabout, and use chalk if you are outdoors or removable coloured plastic tape if you are indoors to define the layout.

As the game develops, suggest that the children have a garage area and a petrol pump. Make a petrol pump using carton boxes with a length of flexible plastic piping stuck into an opening in the side.

Encourage the children to take it in turns to be the garage attendant. The drivers should say 'please' and 'thank you' as they order and fill up with petrol.

Special support
If you have a child who is using sign language, encourage all the children to sign 'please' and 'thank you' in this game, using these Makaton signs (see right). Some children with physical difficulties will find it hard to make signs with precise movements. Instead, accept their approximation of it, perhaps gradually 'shaping up' the sign as they become more skilled.

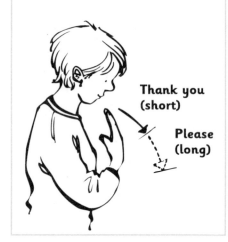

Thank you (short)

Please (long)

Extension
Let older children design road layouts on sheets of paper and play with toy cars.

Send a wish

Group size
Eight to 20 children.

What to do
Use this activity as part of your regular circle time. Sit together in a circle and talk about wishes. Say that most of us can think of something we really wish for and wouldn't it be lovely if our wishes came true? Ask if anyone really wished for something and then it happened. Encourage the children to talk about family occasions, presents that they have received and given, and friends that they have made.

Explain that our wishes do not always come true but that sometimes we can help each other to make wishes come true. Talk about when a child has been feeling sad and their friends made them happy again. Say that perhaps someone wished to have lots of fun with the music and singing in the group today and that the children made it come true.

Suggest that you play a pretending game. Hold up your fist near to your mouth and say something like, 'I wish that the sun would shine!'. Hold your palm flat and gently blow your wish into the air. Take it in turns around the circle to say a wish and blow it gently away. If some children prefer to make a silent wish, that is fine too.

Special support
Practise blowing movements, first by playing a 'feather football' game (two of you trying to blow a feather in opposite directions!), then by blowing coloured ink trails with straws or blowing bubbles.

Extension
Send 'good wishes' to a child in hospital or someone who has moved away. Design a card together and add your names.

LEARNING OBJECTIVES FOR ALL THE CHILDREN
● to be confident to speak in a familiar group
● to have a developing awareness of their own needs, views and feelings and be sensitive to the needs, views and feelings of others.

INDIVIDUAL LEARNING TARGET
● to develop confidence in a familiar group to practise blowing.

LINKS WITH HOME
Be sensitive to any family changes (such as a family breakdown) which might trigger sad thoughts. This does not mean that you should avoid the subject but you might wish to let the child talk about it one to one.

Dress fancy

Group size
Three or four children.

What you need
Fancy-dress clothes to include hats, scarves, boas, shoes, bags and other props; Velcro; needle and thread (adult use); low railing or shelves; full-length wall-mounted mirror, if possible.

What to do
Take a critical look at your dressing-up area:
● Is it inclusive and accessible to all children?
● Does it contain a wide range of clothing reflecting different ethnic groups and cultures?
● Are there clothes attractive to all the children, regardless of their age, stage, gender and preferences?
● Do the adults support the children in non-judgemental ways, without stereotyping (avoiding statements such as 'Boys don't wear pink!')?

Take a look at whether the clothes are accessible to children who have physical and co-ordination difficulties as well. Can you replace buttons with Velcro strips? Can you cut out the back of some of the shoes to make them slip-on? Can you include simple wrap-around cloaks and boas? Have you included huge buttons and straps for practising the finger movements involved in dressing and undressing successfully? Can everything be arranged so that the child with sensory or physical difficulties can still locate and reach for all the items?

Have a grand opening of your new fancy-clothes shop. Set up a mirror for the children to enjoy the effect and a grand parade through your group as they show off their appearances.

Special support
Use this as a natural opportunity for encouraging dressing and undressing skills. For a child with significant physical difficulties, start by encouraging them to pull a light chiffon scarf off their faces and move on to wearing hats and cloaks.

Extension
Introduce a shop mannequin and encourage the children to design a shop-window display.

LEARNING OBJECTIVE FOR ALL THE CHILDREN
● to dress and undress independently.

INDIVIDUAL LEARNING TARGET
● to put on and remove one simple article from the dressing-up box.

LINKS WITH HOME
Link the skills that you are practising with the child's progress at home so that you can each keep up to date with the specific independence skills that the child is learning there.

LEARNING OBJECTIVES FOR ALL THE CHILDREN
- to understand that people have different needs and views
- to understand that they can expect others to treat their needs and views with respect.

INDIVIDUAL LEARNING TARGETS
- to develop positive self-esteem
- to develop confidence in their abilities.

I can!

Group size
Six to 20 children.

What to do
Sit together in a circle and introduce this song, sung to the traditional folk tune of 'Camp Town Races':

> Tell you something I can do,
> Doo – dah, doo – dah,
> Tell you something I can do,
> Doo – dah, doo – dah day!
>
> *Hannah Mortimer*

After the first verse, pause and tell the children something that you can do. 'I can stand on one foot!' (or whatever you choose). Show the children what you can do, and then sing another verse together. Take turns around the circle, each child telling everyone about something that they feel proud about. If they cannot think of something, you tell them each something that you have noticed them do which you are proud of, such as 'I saw you being kind to Jamie when he had fallen over' or 'I like the way you made your sparkly pictures with the glue stick'. Sometimes the suggestions will lend themselves to the child showing something off there and then.

Special support
Talk to any child that you are targeting before the activity and think of a suggestion together – perhaps they have recently learned a new skill or enjoyed a new activity. This will allow you to support the child fluently when it comes to their turn.

Extension
Repeat the game another day by encouraging the children to talk about each other, singing 'Tell you something Zac can do... (and so on)' and then inviting suggestions from the others about all the things that Zac can do.

LINKS WITH HOME
Use this idea to make a celebration song at the end of term, singing it as a group to parents and carers, providing an opportunity to show off creations and successes to them.

LEARNING OBJECTIVE FOR ALL THE CHILDREN
● to form good relationships with adults and peers.

INDIVIDUAL LEARNING TARGET
● to recount one familiar memory in a familiar group when supported.

LINKS WITH HOME
Make sure that all the families are included, being aware of any literacy or language difficulties. Translate the sheet into other languages if necessary, and encourage the sharing of memories from a range of cultures and countries.

Memories

Group size
All the children.

What you need
A little box or carrier bag for each child (plus some spares); sticky labels; felt-tipped pen; memorabilia from home; the photocopiable sheet on page 87.

What to do
Prepare for this activity by bringing in a personal item of memorabilia from home, such as a holiday souvenir, a teddy from your childhood or a photograph. Place it in a box or bag and stick on a label saying 'My memory box/bag'. Make a similar box/bag and label for each child in the group and make a copy of the photocopiable sheet for each child.

Gather the children in a circle or group at the end of the session and introduce your memory box. Ask the children if they know what a memory is and talk about remembering both happy memories and sad memories. Invite the children to tell you what they remember about going on holiday, being a baby, a special event at home or about starting in your group.

Show the children the item in your memory box/bag and tell them why you chose it. Pass it around for each child to look at. Now show the children the memory boxes or bags that you have prepared. Give each child a copy of the photocopiable sheet

and help them to fold it up and place it in their box or bag. Explain that they should take their memory box/bag home and choose something to bring in to the group the next day to talk about 'memories'.

The next day, let the children take it in turns to show what they have brought in and to share their memories. Have a few spare items for any child who has not brought anything in, taking a moment to help them choose something from the setting which 'reminds' them of a memory to share.

Special support
Make a point of talking to parents and carers so that you can share the memory first and support any child who has difficulties in speaking clearly as they 'show and tell'.

Extension
Encourage older children to set up a memory table and use the items on it as talking points.

LEARNING OBJECTIVE FOR ALL THE CHILDREN
● to understand that people have different needs which should be treated with respect.

INDIVIDUAL LEARNING TARGET
● to understand that they can expect others to treat their needs with respect.

Making it easier

Group size
Two or three children.

What you need
A wheelchair (the community occupational therapist, hospital appliances department or a local leisure centre might be able to lend you one); a book such as *Tibby Tried It* by Sharon and Ernie Useman (Magination Press) (see page 95).

What to do
In this activity all the children will have the opportunity to experience wheelchair use and talk about access for wheelchair users. It is suitable for a group of able-bodied children, especially if you are expecting a child who uses a wheelchair to join your setting in the near future. It is also suitable for mixed-ability groups, in which case you can encourage the sharing of ideas and insights.

Lead into the subject of disability by using a story book featuring disability or a child in a wheelchair, such as *Tibby Tried It*. Ideally your picture books will represent a wide range of ability and disability so that this will not be a new topic for the children to think about.

Gather around the wheelchair and talk about how it is used. Ask the children if they know what a wheelchair helps you to do. Explain that some people cannot use their legs to walk and so they need a special chair to help them move around. Invite any child who uses a wheelchair to show theirs off and provide a demonstration.

Let the children take it in turns to be wheeled around your immediate area and talk about whether they can reach the toys and the door handles. Comment on the obstacles on the floor and any steps that block your way. Help the children to begin to understand what could be done to make their group and their community easier for a child in a wheelchair.

Special support
If there is already a wheelchair user in your group, arrange for two wheelchairs to go around together, so that the children can share ideas and suggestions.

Extension
Keep a note of all the children's ideas and talk about them all together, making plans for how to change the position of things in your setting.

LINKS WITH HOME
Use your regular newsletter to encourage parents and carers to help their children think about wheelchair access when they are out and about. They could consider if a certain shop is easy to use or if there is a lift.

LEARNING OBJECTIVE FOR ALL THE CHILDREN
● to respond to significant experiences showing a range of feelings when appropriate.

INDIVIDUAL LEARNING TARGET
● to share laughter in a familiar group.

Laugh along

Group size
Six to eight children.

What you need
A box of funny props such as funny hats, false moustaches, spectacles, red nose and party whistle; some simple jokes to tell.

What to do
Sit down together in a circle for this game in which the children entertain one another and share humour. You may like to reserve this activity until the group has settled well so that the children do not become too excitable or feel threatened in any way.

Start by sharing a simple joke with the children. Most children can usually begin to respond to jokes and humour which involve watching a funny action (such as a funny hat or a silly walk) or imagining something ridiculous ('What's big and yellow? An elephant in a bowl of custard!'). Understanding the double-meaning of more subtle jokes tends to come at a later age.

Now invite the children to take turns at making everyone laugh. Suggest that they look into your box for ideas, or do a funny dance in the middle of the circle. Share an infectious humour as you laugh and applaud together.

Special support
Prepare any child with particular difficulties or needs for this activity by helping them to plan ahead what they would like to do and supporting them as they do it.

Extension
Try keeping straight faces as you challenge a child to make you all laugh (always make sure that you succumb in the end!). Talk together about what makes something funny.

LINKS WITH HOME
Use the 'What's big and yellow?' format to help each child think up a simple joke to share with their parents or carers at home time.

COMMUNICATION, LANGUAGE AND LITERACY

The activities in this chapter encourage language and literacy skills, including letter recognition, word-building, listening to the syllables of words and recognizing rhymes.

Drum beats

Group size
Eight to 20 children.

What you need
A large portable drum (a bodhrán or tambour is ideal); beater.

What to do
Use this activity as a greeting activity. Sit down together in a circle and invite the children to beat their first names on the drum as you say 'Hello' to them. Demonstrate by coming into the centre of the circle and turning to the children next to you. Say, for example, 'Hello Phi-lip', 'Hello Ca-ro-line', 'Hello Ah-med', beating the syllables of their names as you say them.

Now move around the circle, giving the beater to each child in turn, and saying 'Hello...', encouraging them to beat their name to you. Use your expression and your smile to give them clues and encouragement. Praise all the children for joining in.

Special support
You should be able to guarantee total success with this activity, regardless of each child's level of ability. Some children will manage this activity all by themselves, others will need you to whisk the drum away after the correct number of beats and therefore succeed with your help. For children who find it hard to hold a beater, let them use a hand or fist instead, perhaps with a physical prompt (hand over hand) from an adult.

Extension
Older children may be able to tackle their full names with practice. Take your drum to the book corner and invite the children to beat out titles from well-known books. Let them try 'Spot' or 'Top-sy and Tim', or even 'The Ve-ry Hun-gry Cat-ter-pil-lar'!

LEARNING OBJECTIVE FOR ALL THE CHILDREN
● to hear and say short vowel sounds and end sounds within words.

INDIVIDUAL LEARNING TARGET
● to maintain balance when seated by using 'saving' mechanisms.

This way, that way

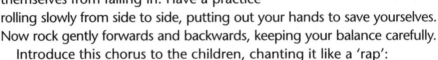

Group size
Six to 12 children.

What to do
Sit down together in a circle on the floor. Tell the children that you are going to pretend to climb aboard a pirate ship. Explain that it might roll about a bit, and ask if they can stop themselves from falling in. Have a practice rolling slowly from side to side, putting out your hands to save yourselves. Now rock gently forwards and backwards, keeping your balance carefully.

Introduce this chorus to the children, chanting it like a 'rap':

> Rolling this way, rolling that way,
> Rocking forwards, rocking back,
> Climbing the rigging and hoisting the tops'l
> All on the ship of Captain Jack!

Repeat it together slowly as you roll slowly from side to side and rock gently forwards and back for the first two lines. You can mime climbing the rigging and hoisting the topsail for the last two lines.

Now introduce the first verse:

> Here comes one! I ate a bun.
> I sailed away round the world and back,
> Climbing the rigging and hoisting the tops'l
> All on the ship of Captain Jack!
>
> *Hannah Mortimer*

Repeat the chorus as you rock and roll. For the second verse, pause at the end of the first line, repeating it a few times and asking the children to suggest a word which sounds like 'two', for example, 'shoe'. As they provide suggestions, repeat the word alongside 'two' and ask them if they sound the same. Agree on the word that you will use and continue.

Here are the suggested final two verses, or you could make up your own variations: 'Here comes three! I climbed a tree' and 'Here comes four! I knocked at the door'. Check if the children are listening by putting in a nonsense word before inviting them to correct you, for example, 'Here comes three! I climbed a... cauliflower'.

Special support
This activity is especially suitable for children just learning sitting balance and 'saving' reactions. The physiotherapist or carer might be able to show you how to gently support the child's balance as they put out hands to save themselves from rocking too far.

Extension
Invite older children to help you make up new verses.

LINKS WITH HOME
Share the rhyme with the parents or carers of a targeted child if rocking exercises are being practised at home.

LEARNING OBJECTIVE FOR ALL THE CHILDREN
● to attempt writing for various purposes to understand that print carries meaning.

INDIVIDUAL LEARNING TARGET
● to compose a short message to a friend.

Dear friend

Group size
One or two children at a time.

What you need
Sheets of paper; envelopes; pencils.

What to do
Choose this activity when one of the children in your group is absent for a long period of time, perhaps because they are in hospital or convalescing at home. Suggest to the children that the child might be missing them, and ask them what they might do to show (child's name) that they are all thinking of him or her. Hopefully someone will suggest sending a letter. Plan together what you will need to write a letter and tell the children that you will help them to do so. Ask them to think what they would like to say and offer to write it down for them. Let them think about what kinds of things they would like to tell their friend and spend some time talking about this in a group to help the children plan and sequence their ideas.

Now move on to a table with one or two of the children and help them to speak in short sentences as you agree together what you will write. Read each sentence back as it is written and encourage the child to read with you as you point to the words. Aim for three or four sentences starting with 'Dear…' and ending with 'From…' (or similar).

At the end, invite each child to add a picture as you work with the next child. Help the children to fold their letters and put them in envelopes.

Special support
This activity has been suggested in order to include a child who might spend periods of time in hospital or home because of their medical condition or because of recent surgery. In the book *Medical Difficulties* by Hannah Mortimer (*Special Needs in the Early Years* series, Scholastic), you will find other ideas for including absent children.

Extension
Encourage older children to write or copy their letters independently.

LINKS WITH HOME
Try to deliver the letters personally and read them through to the absent child.

LEARNING OBJECTIVE FOR ALL THE CHILDREN
● to extend their vocabulary, exploring the meanings and sounds of new words.

INDIVIDUAL LEARNING TARGET
● to make repetitive speech sounds.

LINKS WITH HOME
If you use a regular speech-and-language-therapy home–setting diary, you will all be able to keep in touch with any speech-therapy goals.

Animal fair

Group size
Six to 20 children.

What you need
A set of cards each with the letter sound that you are going to include, such as 'p', 'l', 'b', 'm' and 'z'.

What to do
Many of these activities benefit from a circle-time format because this helps all the children to feel included, allows you to keep eye contact with all the children and use your looks and gestures to keep everyone motivated and confident.

Gather the children together, sitting in a circle, and introduce the song below, to the traditional tune of 'Girls and Boys Come Out to Play', holding up the letter card for 'p' as you sing.

Come and see the animal fair
There's p – p – p – penguins everywhere!
P – p – p – p – p – p –p
P – p – p – penguins everywhere!

Hannah Mortimer

Keep the speed steady to allow the children to enunciate the repeated sounds.

Sing the song together again. Now introduce another letter card, perhaps an 'l' and ask if the children can think of an animal beginning with the letter 'l'. Spend a moment or two exploring their suggestions together as you agree on a good animal to choose. Now sing your own version of the next verse. It might say 'l – l – l – lions everywhere'.

Repeat this for new letter sounds, making up the verses as you go along. You might have 'b – b – b – bears everywhere', 'm – m – m – monkeys everywhere' and 'z – z – z – zebras everywhere'.

Special support
Select speech sounds which a child who has enunciation difficulties might be working on, so that you can use the song as a natural way of reinforcing their learning.

Extension
Sing the song and invite older children to pick out the letter card for the sound that you are singing.

Mr Bear

Group size
Four to 12 children.

What you need
A decorated box; teddy bear; selection of small objects (such as a shell, a button, a ring and a feather).

What to do
Sit down in a circle together and introduce Mr Bear. Take him around the circle and introduce him by name to each child so that he can shake paws. Now make Mr Bear point to the little box in which you have hidden the shell. Say, 'Mr Bear, what have you there?' and take a peep inside the box, without telling the children what you can see. Provide a simple description for the children: 'It's small, hard and white. It has a curly shape. Mr Bear found it at the seaside. It was lying on the sand...'.

Encourage the children to ask Mr Bear questions, and make him shake his head for 'no' and nod for 'yes'. Continue providing more and more clues and information until the children have guessed what is in the box.

Pass the object around the circle for everyone to have a look, repeating the words you used in the description, 'Can you see the *curly* shape?' 'Does it feel *hard*?'.

Repeat for the other items which you have chosen.

Special support
If a child that you are targeting is just learning how to respond to questions that require yes/no answers, let them take a turn at being Mr Bear and support them as they answer the children's questions with a yes/no or a nod/shake.

Extension
Invite older children to provide a description of what is in the box for the other children to guess.

LEARNING OBJECTIVES FOR ALL THE CHILDREN
● to use talk to organize and clarify thinking
● to sustain attentive listening, responding with questions.

INDIVIDUAL LEARNING TARGET
● to indicate a yes/no response.

LINKS WITH HOME
If you are targeting a child at this level of skill, suggest that the parents or carers continue to teach a yes/no response at home by offering choices wherever possible: 'Would you like *milk* (pause for response) or *juice* (pause for response)?'.

Robot Rita

Group size
Six to 20 children.

What you need
An additional adult helper; clear floor space, indoors or outdoors.

What to do
Explain this activity to the adult who is helping you before you begin. Invite the children to move into your floor space and to enjoy pretending to be robots for a few moments, moving with stiff limbs. Now invite the children to sit down in a row at one end of your open space. Tell them that you are going to be a robot but that they should 'program' you. Explain that you can only move if the children tell you to, you can take steps forwards and then stop (demonstrate), you can take steps backwards and then stop (demonstrate), and that is all you can do.

Stand still while your helper consults with the children. They should agree together on how many steps you are going to take, and the helper should ask the children to shout 'Stop!' when you have taken that many. 'The children want you to take three steps forwards'. Take three large steps as the children count out loud with your helper and then shout 'Stop!'. Continue for a while, following the children's group instructions.

Your helper should then invite individual children to take a turn at directing you.

Special support
Some children with, for example, cerebral palsy take a while to process information and to communicate what they are thinking in a fluid way. They might enjoy commanding you to 'Go!' and to 'Stop!' even if they cannot co-ordinate this fluently with counting the steps that you take. Give them the opportunity (and the self-prestige) to control your movement in this way.

Extension
You could introduce 'rights' and 'lefts' with older children.

LEARNING OBJECTIVE FOR ALL THE CHILDREN
● to speak clearly and audibly with confidence and control and show awareness of the listener.

INDIVIDUAL LEARNING TARGET
● to call out 'Stop!'.

LINKS WITH HOME
The child that you are targeting might enjoy remote-controlling electronic toys at home, perhaps using a specially-adapted switch device suitable for the movements that they are capable of controlling (see page 96).

Journey to the bottom of the sea

Group size
Six to 12 children.

LEARNING OBJECTIVE FOR ALL THE CHILDREN
● to use language to imagine and re-create roles and experiences.

INDIVIDUAL LEARNING TARGET
● to show enjoyment of role-play and to participate, even if only passively.

What you need
An ocean drum; rainmaker; basin of water; blowing tube; glockenspiel (or similar).

What to do
Place your props safely to one side of you and sit down together in a circle. Explain to the children that you are going to tell them a story. Say that you are going to pretend to take a journey down to the bottom of the sea. What do the children think you will see there? What might they hear there? Ask them to sit comfortably while you talk. Invite older children to close their eyes as they listen.

You are walking on a beach. It is sandy and gravelly. Can you feel the stones between your toes? Listen to the crunching sound you make as you walk (move the rainmaker to make the sounds of footsteps in the sand). *You are approaching the edge of the sea. Can you hear the waves* (swirl the ocean drum gently)*? Into the water you go. You are pleased to find out it is really warm. Can you feel the water lapping all around you? Suddenly, you discover that you are magic and that you can breathe under the water. Down you go, walking along the sea bed. Can you hear the gurgling sound of the water?* (blow bubbles gently through your tube into your basin of water).

Continue with the story and develop it along the lines of the children's suggestions.

Special support
You can use this kind of visualization to encourage relaxation and steady breathing for a child whose movements or spasm make them jerky and tense. As you introduce the waves and the rainmaker, encourage all the children to breathe slowly in and out with the sounds that you are making. Breathe in and out to the rhythm of the waves, taking slightly longer to breathe out than in.

Extension
Try other sound stories, relaxation and visualization techniques. For further ideas, see *More Quality Circle Time* by Jenny Mosley (see page 95).

LINKS WITH HOME
If you can teach the children to take slow breaths, this is an excellent skill to share with home in order to encourage the children to relax or to control hot tempers. Send a copy of the photocopiable sheet on page 88 home with each child.

LEARNING OBJECTIVES FOR ALL THE CHILDREN
● to link sounds to letters, naming and sounding the letters of the alphabet
● to word-build their own names.

INDIVIDUAL LEARNING TARGET
● to recognize their name.

Who am I?

Group size
Three or four children.

What you need
A board approximately 1m x 1m; fabric or felt; staple gun (adult use); small stick-on patches of Velcro (approximately 1cm x 1cm); cards (approximately 5cm x 5cm); felt-tip; glue.

What to do
Make the felt board, which will be useful for many other activities, such as 'Story felts' on page 43. Ask your nearest haberdashery to advise you on the best fabrics for using with Velcro. Cover the board with the fabric and use a staple gun on the reverse side to hold it in position.

Now make a series of cards, each with one letter on. Make a set of upper-case letters and a set of lower-case letters. If any of the children have more than one of the same letter in their names, you will need enough letter cards for them to be able to each build up their name. On the reverse side of each card, glue the smooth side of a small patch of Velcro. You will be able to use these letter

cards again and again for a range of early literacy activities.

Gather the children around you and show them the board and a small selection of the letter cards. Place the letters for one of the children's first names in a jumbled-up arrangement on the board and invite them to rearrange the letters to form their name. Do the same for all the children in turn. Encourage them to sound the letters out as they handle them.

Special support
To make this activity easier, arrange all the letters of the child's name on the board in the correct sequence, with the first letter missing. Offer a choice of two letters and ask the child which one should go at the beginning of their name. In time, you can increase the choice and make the task more difficult. Even if a child cannot manipulate the cards, they might be able to indicate which letter you should use from a choice.

Extension
Older children can select the letter cards themselves from a selection on a table, or word-build their whole names or a short phrase.

LINKS WITH HOME
Send plain letter cards (without Velcro) home in an envelope and ask parents and carers to encourage their children to build up their names by arranging the letters in the correct order.

Story felts

Group size
Three or four children.

What you need
Felt board (see page 42); card; scissors; coloured felt; glue; patches of Velcro; A3 copy of the photocopiable sheet on page 89; copy of *Red Riding Hood* (Ladybird Books).

What to do
Introduce the story by reading the book to the children. Cut a copy of the A3 photocopiable sheet into five sections and give each child one section to colour. Colour one yourself too and talk about the story of Red Riding Hood as you work together. Cut out the characters carefully and stick them on to sheets of card. When the characters are dry, encourage the children to cut the card around them. Stick the smooth side of a Velcro patch to the rear of each character and place them all on one side to dry.

Later, gather around the felt board and re-create the story of Red Riding Hood using the characters that you have cut out. Read the story again, sticking the different characters to the felt board as the story progresses.

During later sessions, encourage the children to make up their own stories, or versions of familiar stories, creating their own characters to mount on to card and use with the felt board.

Special support
Even if a child's manipulative skills are poor, encourage them to take an active part in deciding how the story should progress and what characters to mount next on the felt board.

Extension
Ask older children to help you make story characters using shapes of coloured felt stuck on to card.

LEARNING OBJECTIVES FOR ALL THE CHILDREN
● to enjoy listening to and using spoken language
● to use talk to sequence and clarify thinking.

INDIVIDUAL LEARNING TARGET
● to make choices as to what happens next in a story.

LINKS WITH HOME
Make up a book to tell a story that the children have invented and invite individual children to borrow it to take home and share with their families.

Getting a grip

Group size
Two or three children.

What you need
A selection of pencils, some chubby and some thinner; a few triangular pencils; selection of pencil grips (see page 96); felt-tipped pen; paper.

What to do
Start by exploring the pencils together and finding one that seems to suit each child. Children at early stages of developing the correct pencil grip (the 'tripod grip', using two fingers and one thumb) will benefit from using a triangular chubby pencil or a triangular pencil grip around an ordinary pencil. Place it near the lead end of the pencil for better control. Play a game holding your pencils in the air and pretending writing in the air, holding the pencil correctly.

Next, challenge the children to keep holding their pencils correctly as they scribble on to paper, first backwards and forwards, then round and round. Keep this part of the activity fun and end on a successful and positive note.

At a later session, take this skill further by inviting each child to join to marks that you make on their paper with your pen. You could draw a bee and a flower and ask the child to join them. You could draw a rabbit and a tree to be joined, or a dog and a bone. Choose your pictures to match the child's particular interest.

Special support
If a child loses the correct grip, gently use your hand over theirs to re-establish it. Aim to keep this activity particularly motivating and enjoyable if a child has fine-motor difficulties. Consult the occupational therapist if you feel that you need more specialist aids or if you are not clear about whether a child is left- or right-handed by the time they are four years old. For left-handed children, place the paper slightly to the left of the centre of their body, ready for the correct writing position later (see page 96).

Extension
Play a game in which you draw two dots on a piece of paper and ask a child to join them. The child then draws two dots on the same piece of paper which you join, but without touching any existing lines. As the game progresses, finer and finer precision is required.

LEARNING OBJECTIVE FOR ALL THE CHILDREN
● to use a pencil and hold it effectively.

INDIVIDUAL LEARNING TARGET
● to hold a pencil in the correct tripod grip.

LINKS WITH HOME
Use your regular newsletter to provide ideas for parents and carers to encourage their children to adopt the correct pencil hold at home.

MATHEMATICAL DEVELOPMENT

Help the children to understand the early language of mathematics and encourage early counting and number recognition. These activities will help you to ensure that children with physical difficulties can be successfully included in the group.

Towering high

Group size
Two groups of four children.

What you need
A set of about eight empty boxes or cartons ranging in size from approximately 5cm³ to 20cm³; wrapping paper; scissors; sticky tape.

What to do
A natural opportunity for this activity might arise if you are preparing a display for a major festival involving the giving and receiving of presents, for example, preparing a display for Santa's grotto.

Cut the sheets of wrapping paper into eight sizes, with the largest big enough to wrap the largest box, and the smallest sheet sufficient for the smallest box.

Gather the first group of children together and spread four boxes and corresponding sheets out on the floor. Talk about their sizes as you arrange them in size order, placing each box on the sheet of paper in which it will be wrapped. Have fun together wrapping and sticking the presents. You will have to provide plenty of help but try to work as a team with the children. Repeat for the second group of children and the remaining four boxes.

When your boxes are wrapped, challenge the children, in pairs, to stack them with the largest at the bottom and the smallest at the top.

Special support
Sometimes children with physical and co-ordination difficulties are denied the opportunity to develop the control needed in placing and stacking a tower because the materials that we offer them are too small. This activity provides an opportunity for them to learn about building towers and develop the language of size with *large* building materials. Choose a size of box which suits the child's level of skill, and hold the bottom box or boxes steady as the child places each into position.

Extension
Provide older children with miniature wrapped boxes and challenge them to stack these.

LEARNING OBJECTIVES FOR ALL THE CHILDREN
● to use developing mathematical ideas to solve a practical problem
● to use words such as 'bigger' and 'smaller' to describe solid shapes.

INDIVIDUAL LEARNING TARGET
● to stack one large block on top of another.

LINKS WITH HOME
Lend some stacking foam blocks to the family of the child that you are targeting so that they can practise stacking, counting and size-grading at home.

LEARNING OBJECTIVE FOR ALL THE CHILDREN
● to use everyday words to describe position.

INDIVIDUAL LEARNING TARGET
● to say and respond to the word 'down'.

Down at the bottom

Group size
Eight to 16 children.

What you need
Any special equipment that the targeted children need for lying on their tummies, such as wedges or beanbags.

What to do
Gather together in a large circle and make sure that you are all at the same level. If one of the children must sit to join in, then everyone should sit or kneel.

Start with the well-known rhyme 'Ring-o-Ring-o-Roses':

Ring-o-Ring-o-Roses, a pocket full of posies;
Atishoo, atishoo, we all fall down!
(Traditional)

If all the children are ambulant, you can hold hands and move around in a circle as you sing, crouching down to the ground at the end. This song also works well if you sit or kneel: dance your hands up in the air, bringing them down to the ground for 'down!'.

Move yourselves into position where you are all lying on your tummies with your heads towards the centre of the circle. Swim with your arms as you chant:

> Down at the bottom of the deep blue sea,
> Catching fishes for my tea.
> How many fishes can you see?
> One, two, three!
>
> *Hannah Mortimer*

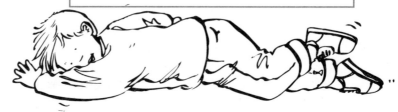

On the count of three, move your bodies up again, back into your sitting, kneeling or standing positions.

Special support
This is an opportunity for a targeted child to practise lying prone on a wedge, if this is one of their physiotherapy exercises. Encourage them to join in with the 'down' as they lower their hands and body.

Extension
You can also use the chant to practise a one–two rhythm as the children pat the ground with alternate hands. Follow up with 'Cobbler, Cobbler, Mend My Shoe' (Traditional).

LINKS WITH HOME
If a child has to undergo regular physiotherapy exercises at home, try to find rhymes that go with the movements to make them more enjoyable.

LEARNING OBJECTIVE FOR ALL THE CHILDREN
● to say and use number names in order.

INDIVIDUAL LEARNING TARGET
● to roll over.

Five in a bed

Group size
Five children.

What you need
A carpeted floor space suitable for the children to lie and roll on; bedspread or duvet.

What to do
Spread the bedspread or duvet on the floor and invite the children to take their shoes off and lie down side by side along the length of it.

Introduce an adaptation of the traditional rhyme 'There Were Ten in the Bed':

> There were five in the bed,
> And the little one said,
> 'Roll over! Roll over!'
> So they all rolled over
> And one fell out. (...)
> So there were four in the bed,...

When you get to the first 'Roll over!', encourage all the children to roll over in the same direction, and help the child at the end as they 'fall off' the bed and sit to one side.

Continue the song until there is only 'one in the bed'. You can then build the number up again by singing:

> ... 'Roll back! Roll back!',
> So they all rolled back and one got in...

Encourage everyone to roll in the opposite direction this time and add one child to the duvet each verse, until you have all five back in your bed!

Special support
This is an opportunity for encouraging a child that you are targeting who is learning to roll over. If a child has dyspraxic difficulties, help them to concentrate on rolling safely, and praise them for not knocking their neighbours.

Extension
Make a model 'five in a bed' out of a shoebox. Make a material cover into which to pop five little people made from pegs.

LINKS WITH HOME
Carers can show you how to support a child who has little movement and control as they roll and turn.

Number flowers

Group size
Three or four children.

What you need
Number-flower cards, some blank and some with pictures to match on to (see diagram below); laminator; matching small toys and plastic shapes.

What to do
Make a set of number flowers on A4 card following the diagram, each with a central number and a set of five or six petals, each containing a set of pictures corresponding to the number (for example, two cars, two buttons, and so on). Start by working on number flowers 1, 2 and 3, then extend up to 5. Laminate the finished cards. Invite the children to match real objects to the

pictures on the petals to make several sets of the chosen numeral. You can also make a number of blank number flowers, each with a numeral in the centre, but with the petals left blank for the children to make up their own sets of whatever the numeral is independently.

Once the children understand what is required of them, encourage them to work independently and to call you to see when they have finished placing all the objects on to their number flowers.

LEARNING OBJECTIVES FOR ALL THE CHILDREN
● to recognize numerals 1 to 5
● to count reliably up to five objects.

INDIVIDUAL LEARNING TARGET
● to 'remember all we have learned about' 1, 2 and 3.

LINKS WITH HOME
Send a number-flower card home for the children to practise and to show their parents or carers what they can do.

Special support
This activity represents numbers and sets visually, and this approach is particularly helpful for children with dyspraxia. Start with number flowers for 1 and 2 and then extend upwards. Use larger flowers and materials if the child has fine-motor difficulties.

Extension
Make larger number flowers up to 10. Invite older children to draw around plastic shapes in order to make number-flower cards for the other children.

LEARNING OBJECTIVE FOR ALL THE CHILDREN
● to recognize and use numerals 1 to 9.

INDIVIDUAL LEARNING TARGET
● to write the numeral 1 with appropriate pencil pressure.

LINKS WITH HOME
Suggest to parents and carers that they try black scraper boards or 'copper art', which can be obtained from art shops. They can be scraped using a special nib with a fairly strong pressure to make white or shiny designs and will help children improve a light pencil pressure. 'Magic slates' are inexpensive toys which provide a similar opportunity.

Carbon copies

Group size
Two children at a time.

What you need
Sheets of A4 paper and A4 carbon paper (use old pads of carbonized paper if available); pencils; pencil grips.

What to do
Make sure that each child has the type of pencil and grip which works best for them (see 'Getting a grip' on page 44). Ask the children to put on aprons as working with carbon paper can be messy.

Make a game out of writing numerals on to the top copy and then seeing what has come through on to the second sheet, using carbon paper in between. See how many numerals each child can write, following your dictation, and use the results as an assessment opportunity.

Next, whisper a 'secret number' to one child (such as 4) and invite them to write it 'secretly' on to their top copy. Ask them to pass the second copy to their partner and then see if their partner can guess the number from what has been written. Ask the first child to check their copy and see if this is correct.

Use the game as an opportunity for the children to practise writing numerals to dictation.

Special support
This activity is particularly helpful for children with light pencil pressure. Challenge them to see how many layers of paper and carbon they can make a mark through. Start with a single vertical stroke for the numeral 1. Experiment with circular scribbles and horizontal lines too.

Extension
Use the carbon copying paper as a resource for a role-play office corner. In addition, provide money for the children to count and envelopes for them to send out bills!

LEARNING OBJECTIVE FOR ALL THE CHILDREN
● to talk about, recognize and re-create simple patterns.

INDIVIDUAL LEARNING TARGETS
● to match colours one to one
● to copy a simple pattern.

LINKS WITH HOME
Ask parents and carers to encourage their children to make patterns using pegboards, mosaic boards and coloured bricks at home.

Mix and match

Group size
Two or three children.

What you need
Coloured pens; coloured one-inch cubes; laminator.

What to do
Make a worksheet with templates of squares as shown below and make copies to provide one for each child and about ten spare copies. On the spare copies, colour the two squares on the top left with two different-coloured pens, so that they match some of the one-inch cubes that you have in your setting. You can mix and match the colours so that each sheet has different combinations of colours. Repeat for the bottom left figure, selecting different colours for the three squares. Leave the templates on the right side of the page blank. Laminate the sheets at this stage if you wish.

Working with a small group of children, provide the laminated coloured-in sheets and a choice of one-inch cubes in colours to match the colours on the sheets. Encourage the children to place the cubes in the correct positions on the sheets, first covering the shapes on the left, and then re-creating the same patterns on the right with some more cubes. Repeat with the other sheets.

Next, give each child a copy of the worksheet and oversee them as they colour in the left side of the sheet with colours of their choice. Invite them to invent and play their own version of this matching game. Encourage them to work independently if they can, showing you what they have achieved at the end.

Special support
Template-matching and copying activities are particularly helpful for children with dyspraxia. Quite often, these children also have perceptual difficulties and benefit from practice in visual discrimination and matching. Further ideas for activities like this can be found in Madeleine Portwood's book (see page 95) and also in *Write From the Start* (see page 96).0

Extension
Make more complex templates, perhaps with three squares arranged in an 'L' shape, or grids of 3 x 3 squares.

LEARNING OBJECTIVE FOR ALL THE CHILDREN
● to respond to everyday words describing position.

INDIVIDUAL LEARNING TARGET
● to respond to 'on' and 'under'.

Just do it!

Group size
Six to 12 children.

What to do
Sit or stand in a circle together and enjoy a familiar action rhyme featuring body parts, such as 'Heads, Shoulders, Knees and Toes' or 'Put Your Finger On Your Head', both in Okki-tokki-unga (A & C Black). Make sure that the children can identify the parts of their bodies.

Next, sit down and ask the children to 'put your hands *under* your legs' or 'put your chin *on* your knees'. Let them think about this for a moment and then add the challenge 'Just… do it!'.

Think of some other challenges involving the key words 'on' and 'under', such as 'Put your hands *on* your head', 'Put your fingers *under* your chin' and so on. Share the humour as you move your bodies into new positions.

Finish by moving into a large space and challenging the children in the same way to go *under* the table, *on* the mat, *behind* the piano and so on, as appropriate.

Special support
Body action games are helpful for children with dyspraxia who have poor body awareness. Start by keeping the game very simple, asking them to 'touch your *elbow*', 'touch your *knee*' and so on, and then begin to introduce pairs of body parts and positional words.

Extension
Older children might be able to respond to instructions involving right and left: 'Put your *right* hand on your *left* foot', 'Put your *right* elbow on your *left* knee' and so on. Allow the children to take turns setting the challenges for other children.

LINKS WITH HOME
If children have difficulty remembering the names of parts of the body, ask parents and carers to spend time teaching the correct names using a favourite teddy or cuddly toy.

My tower, your tower

Group size
Two children at a time.

What you need
One-inch coloured blocks for stacking; nine card discs, each two inches in diameter; felt-tipped pen.

What to do
Write one numeral from 1 to 9 on each of the nine card discs.

Working with two children at a time, build a small tower of three blocks on a table. Now give one of the children three similar blocks. Count the blocks together, arranging them in a line and touching one block at a time to encourage one-to-one correspondence. Invite the child to copy your tower beside it. Count the blocks again. Is the number still the same? (Older children might be able to explain why.) Celebrate their success. Encourage the child to choose the correct card disc to balance carefully on top of the tower, showing how many blocks there are in the tower. Repeat with the other child.

Try some more towers, staying approximately within and slightly beyond each child's level of skill. So if the child can build a four-block tower confidently but has difficulty with a six-block tower, stay with four, five or six blocks.

It does not matter what colour blocks are used to make the towers, but the children should aim to make towers of the same height.

Special support
If a child has fine-motor difficulties, use larger blocks and card discs. Steady the bottom blocks, if you need to, as the child places the top blocks into position. Encourage them to build their own towers up to their level of skill. If they are counting well but cannot co-ordinate the building of a tower, then place the blocks for them as they count.

Extension
Challenge older children to copy the colour sequence as well as the quantity of blocks.

LEARNING OBJECTIVES FOR ALL THE CHILDREN
● to count reliably up to six
● to talk about one more or one less than a number from one to five.

INDIVIDUAL LEARNING TARGET
● to balance on one leg for three seconds.

One-legged Sam

Group size
Six to 20 children.

What you need
An open floor space, indoors or outdoors.

What to do
Stand in the open space and introduce this chant:

> One-legged Sam the pirate man
> Sailed to sea in an old tin can;
> He was a terrifying fellow
> With fearsome looks and a mighty bellow.
> Stand on one leg if you can,
> Copy Sam the pirate man!
>
> *Hannah Mortimer*

Repeat the chant together, with actions. Make up ferocious expressions for the third line and pause to bellow 'Land ahoy!' after the fourth. At the end of the rhyme, ask the children to try standing on one leg as you all count to six. See how long they manage to stay balanced for! Repeat the chant, this time balancing on the other leg at the end of the rhyme.

Invite individual children to balance on one leg as the rest of you count out loud. Compare your counts. Who could balance for four? Who stayed up for six? Who had one more than three? Try again and stay up for one more and so on.

Special support
Offer children with dyspraxia a steadying finger to help them balance. Let them practise balancing skills by trying to walk heel-to-toe along a chalk line. If a child is non-ambulant and cannot balance, then encourage them to lead the counting.

LINKS WITH HOME
Children with dyspraxia can benefit from trying these activities at home: encouraged by their parents or carers, they could practise walking on toes, on heels, on the insides of their feet, and then on the outsides of their feet.

Extension
Older children might be able to maintain their one-legged balance throughout the rhyme.

LEARNING OBJECTIVES FOR ALL THE CHILDREN
● to count reliably to six objects
● to talk about one more or one less than a number from 1 to 5.

INDIVIDUAL LEARNING TARGET
● to roll a ball and knock over a skittle.

Knocked for six

Group size
Four children.

What you need
A set of plastic skittles; plastic ball; large foam balls.

What to do
Encourage the children to wear loose clothing or tracksuits, and wear trousers or a loose skirt yourself, so that you can all sit on the floor with your legs splayed.

Start by teaching the children how to roll and aim a ball. Ask them to sit down opposite one another in an open floor space with their legs wide apart, and show them how to roll the large foam balls between them, funnelling the ball in the right direction.

When all the children can roll the balls with approximate aim, set up three of the skittles about ten feet away. Take it in turns to roll the plastic ball towards the skittles until you have knocked all three over (this stops the game becoming competitive as you are working as a team).

Count the skittles as they fall. Ask questions such as, 'How many more do we need to knock over?', 'How many did Chad knock down?', 'How many throws did it take to knock them all down?' and so on. Look for natural opportunities to reinforce counting and for the children to think about 'one more than…' and 'one less than…'.

Build up the number of skittles to six, adding one more each time.

Special support
Use a gentle arm-over-arm support to help the children with the rolling activity and the aiming if necessary.

Extension
Play with ten skittles. Challenge the children to knock all ten down in just three throws.

LINKS WITH HOME
Show the parents or carers of a child that you are targeting how to teach simple aiming and rolling at home. Suggest that they use a large foam ball and sit with legs splayed in a 'V' to funnel the ball. Start with large balls, and then refine the skill to smaller balls.

KNOWLEDGE AND UNDERSTANDING OF THE WORLD

These activities will help the children to find out about the world around them, with ideas to include children who have difficulties in physical co-ordination or mobility.

Building site

Group size
Six to 12 children.

What you need
A large sheet of paper; pen; selection of percussion instruments such as wood block and beater, claves, maracas, cymbals, bongo drum and guiro.

What to do
This activity could fit in with the topic of 'Homes' or when the children have noticed a building site near your premises.

Gather the children together on the floor and talk about the process of building a house. What would they need to build a house? What would they have to do? Talk about digging the foundations, pouring the cement, mixing the mortar, laying the bricks, erecting the scaffolding, putting on the roof timbers, laying the tiles, putting the glass into windows, connecting electricity and water, and painting and decorating. Draw pictures as the children volunteer ideas, then use your drawings to help them get the sequences in the right order.

Once the children have decided on the sequence of activities, pass around the instruments and tell the story of how a house is built, adding sound effects. Invite the children to make suggestions of which instruments they could use for the various procedures. They might suggest a drum beat, claves or wooden block for the joiner hammering the nails, the maracas for the cement mixer, and a scratchy guiro for sawing the wood.

Special support
Use this as an opportunity for encouraging a child to use a two-handed instrument if that is a skill that you are targeting. The instruments will provide a range of opportunities for practising different finger and hand skills.

Extension
Draw on cards a picture sequence of a house being built and ask the children to arrange these in the correct order.

LEARNING OBJECTIVES FOR ALL THE CHILDREN
● to find out about and identify the uses of everyday technology
● to observe, find out about and identify features in the place they live and their environment.

INDIVIDUAL LEARNING TARGETS
● to beat two instruments together
● to shake an instrument
● to beat a drum with a hand.

LINKS WITH HOME
Ask parents and carers to walk past a building site with their children and talk about what is happening there.

KNOWLEDGE & UNDERSTANDING OF THE WORLD

LEARNING OBJECTIVE FOR ALL THE CHILDREN
● to observe, find out and identify features of their own bodies and how they work.

INDIVIDUAL LEARNING TARGET
● to point to four body parts.

Heads and shoulders

Group size
Eight to ten children.

What to do
Gather the children in a circle, standing up. If the child that you are targeting can only sit or lie, then ask all the children to adopt a similar position so that you are all on the same level. This activity shows how a very familiar rhyme or song can be adapted to include all children regardless of their needs.

Use this well-known rhyme:

> Heads, shoulders, knees and toes, knees and toes,
> Heads, shoulders, knees and toes, knees and toes,
> And eyes and ears and mouth and nose,
> Heads, shoulders, knees and toes, knees and toes.
> (Traditional)

Start very slowly, and allow most of the children to join in independently from the start, copying your actions as you point to each body part on yourself. Pair any child who is still learning body parts with an adult to help. The first time through, the helper should point to each part mentioned on the child, emphasizing the key word, 'Head… shoulder... knee... toes... eye… ear... mouth… nose…'.

The second time through, take it just as slowly, but ask the helpers to encourage (with a hand-over-hand support if necessary) the children to point to themselves.

The third time through, take it at as fast as you can, just for fun! The helpers should do the pointing again on to their children, ending with a laugh and a tickle. Meanwhile, the children who are able to join in the activity independently will have the challenge of doing so very quickly.

Special support
If a child finds physical control very difficult, let the adult touch their body as the child hears the word for each body part. Take it slowly enough at first for the child to use eye-pointing to anticipate which part comes next. Look for any sign of anticipation and praise it. If a child has rushed and impulsive movements, then starting this rhyme slowly and steadily should help them to gain more control.

Extension
Add in different body parts to the song 'If You're Happy and You Know It', such as 'Touch your ankle' and so on.

LINKS WITH HOME
If a child is still learning body parts, ask the parents or carers to practise four simple parts with their child at home by asking them to 'show me your hand, foot, head and tummy'.

LEARNING OBJECTIVES FOR ALL THE CHILDREN
● to find out about trains
● to construct a group train

INDIVIDUAL LEARNING TARGET
● to take part actively in a familiar role play.

LINKS WITH HOME
Invite the children to bring in their favourite stories about Thomas the Tank Engine from home to share with the group. Repeat the game with the new set of characters.

Express train

Group size
Six to eight children.

What you need
A chair for each child and one for yourself; guard's flag and whistle; driver's hat; picture book about Thomas the Tank Engine.

What to do
Ask the children if they enjoy stories about Thomas the Tank Engine and share the picture book that you have chosen, talking about your favourite characters.

Arrange the chairs in a 'train', one behind the other, and encourage the children to help move them into position. Suggest that you all travel on a pretend train journey. Ask who would like to be the driver first, and let them wear a hat and sit on the front chair. Invite a child to be the guard. Give them a flag and a whistle, and ask them to sit on the back chair. Start the role-play.

Pretend that you have stopped in a station and passengers are getting off and new ones getting on. Check that all the doors are closed. Is it safe to go? Encourage the guard to blow the whistle and wave the flag.

As the 'train' moves along, move your arms slowly round and round as if they were heavy pistons. Chant rhythmically as you move, starting very slowly and softly, then building up the speed and the volume, ready for the final 'whistle' of 'JAMES!'. On the final word, raise one hand into the air as if you were sounding the steam whistle.

> Percy, Percy, Percy, Percy
> Fat Controller, Fat Controller, Fat Controller, Fat Controller,
> Annie and Clarabel, Annie and Clarabel,
> Annie and Clarabel, Annie and Clarabel,
> Thomas the Engine, Thomas the Engine, Thomas the Engine,
> Thomas the Engine,
> J – A – M – E – SSSSSSS!

Pretend that you have stopped in a station. Have two or three more turns, changing the driver and the guard each time.

Special support
This activity is an excellent way of fully including a child who is in a wheelchair or special seat. It also provides a natural way of practising blowing for a child who has difficulties in co-ordinating mouth movements.

Extension
Challenge older children to think of other names of characters that they could build into a train chant.

Wheels

Group size
Four to six children.

What you need
A book about wheels or wheeled transport, such as *Wheels* by Shirley Hughes (Walker books); book corner; selection of nursery toys; display area.

What to do
Gather the children together and talk about wheels. Share your picture book together. Encourage the children to say what items have wheels, what wheels help us to do and to count how many wheels they can see in the picture book.

Next, look around the room and ask the children to identify anything which has wheels on it in the room (or the play area if you are outside). Talk about the wheeled toys and have an expedition around the area, counting wheels as you go. Ask questions such as, 'How many wheels are there on that (toy) car?', 'How many are there on the tricycle?' and so on.

Now move to the book corner and challenge the children to find a picture of something with wheels on. Collect your pictures and a selection of objects together and place them on a display table.

Special support
Talk about any wheelchair in your setting. Ask questions such as, 'How many wheels does it have?', 'What do the wheels help (Sammie) do?' and so on. Make sure that your book corner contains picture books which include differently-abled children and alternative forms of mobility.

Extension
Use notepads and pencils to make tally marks for each wheel seen in a play area or picture book.

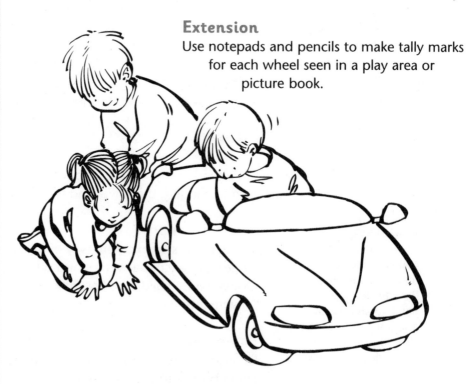

LEARNING OBJECTIVES FOR ALL THE CHILDREN
● to find out about, and identify, some features of things they observe
● to ask questions about how things work.

INDIVIDUAL LEARNING TARGET
● to talk about the wheels on their wheelchair and think about how they move.

LINKS WITH HOME
Talk about how the children came to the setting today. Who travelled on wheels? Who travelled on legs? Send a copy of the photocopiable sheet on page 90 home for parents and carers to enjoy with their children.

Toe to toe

Group size
Eight to 20 children.

What to do
Sit down together in a circle and sing an action song about body parts, such as 'Heads, Shoulders, Knees and Toes' or 'Put Your finger On Your Head' both in Okki-tokki-unga (A & C Black). Challenge the children to 'Wave your arms', 'Tap your knee', 'Wiggle your toes' and so on in order to make sure that they understand the names of the body parts that you are going to use during this activity.

Now challenge the children to enjoy this circle game. Turn to the child on your left and touch your elbow to theirs. Encourage them while they 'pass' the elbow-to-elbow touch on to their neighbour on the left side, touching elbows gently. In this way, pass the elbow-to-elbow touch all the way around the circle.

Next time, turn to your right and touch toes to toes. Encourage the children to pass the toe-to-toe touch all around the circle again. You can continue with a back-to-back touch, a knee-to-knee touch, a palm-to-palm touch and even a heel-to-heel touch. Praise the children for being gentle with each other.

Special support
Sit next to any child that you are targeting for physical and co-ordination difficulties so that you can support them if you need to as they move into different positions and postures.

Extension
Older children can enjoy passing one touch one way round the circle, at the same time managing another touch in the opposite direction!

LEARNING OBJECTIVE FOR ALL THE CHILDREN
● to identify some features of living things.

INDIVIDUAL LEARNING TARGETS
● to identify three body parts
● to move body parts with co-ordination and control.

LINKS WITH HOME
Encourage parents and carers to help their children learn the names of body parts by looking into a mirror together or touching each other's noses, ears and so on.

LEARNING OBJECTIVE FOR ALL THE CHILDREN
● to find out about, and identify, some features of living things.

INDIVIDUAL LEARNING TARGET
● to draw a line with control.

LINKS WITH HOME
Ask parents and carers to help their children prepare for a 'talk about' session on any pets they have. They should help their children to prepare where their pets live and how they help look after them.

At home

Group size
Three or four children.

What you need
A copy of the photocopiable sheet on page 91 for each child; pencils; crayons; pictures of creatures and habitats.

What to do
Gather the children together and encourage them to talk about homes. Ask who lives in a house or a flat. Who lives in a nest? What *does* live in a nest? What lives in a hole in the ground? Talk about different animals and where they live, and introduce some of the correct vocabulary for habitats, such as 'burrow', 'hibernate', 'den' and 'web'. If you have suitable pictures, share these.

Sit at a table and give each child a copy of the photocopiable sheet. Can they draw a line from each animal to the place where it lives? Encourage the children to draw lines from the rabbit to its burrow, from the bird to its nest, the squirrel to its hole in a tree, the hedgehog to its pile of leaves and the spider to its web.

Talk together about the creatures and their habitats as you work. If the children would like to, let them finish by colouring the pictures in or over.

Special support
This activity provides more pencil-control practice following on from 'Getting a grip' on page 44. Help the child to establish the correct pencil grip before they start, and provide a gentle hand-over-hand support to aid pencil control if necessary.

Extension
Go on an expedition around your outdoor area to find minibeasts. Talk about their habitats and take care not to disturb them.

KNOWLEDGE & UNDERSTANDING OF THE WORLD

LEARNING OBJECTIVE FOR ALL THE CHILDREN
● to find out about past and present events in their own lives, and in those of their families and other people they know.

INDIVIDUAL LEARNING TARGET
● to remember a discussion and recall the main ideas.

Mind maps

Group size
Four to ten children.

What you need
A flipchart (or large sheet of paper); coloured pens.

What to do
Use this approach whenever you are having a discussion about a new topic, particularly if you have a child who has dyspraxic or memory difficulties in your group. As you talk, or as the children contribute ideas, try to find a way of representing the keywords visually on the sheet of paper. Make associations between them using arrows. This device helps memories and facts to become 'fixed' without the need for the children to remember all the words that went with them.

The example illustrated below represents a discussion, 'All about me', in which a child might talk about what it would have been like when they were a baby. They might mention needing a pushchair, drinking from a bottle and needing to wear a nappy. All these can be represented in pictures drawn by an adult around the central picture of a baby.

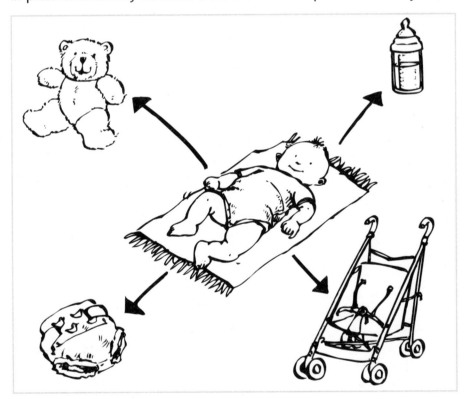

Special support
Mind maps of your present topic work are good ways of helping a child with dyspraxia or memory difficulties to remember what you have talked about. You will find more ideas (developed from Buzan's work) in Madeleine Portwood's book (see page 95).

Extension
Invite older children to begin to draw their own mind maps of ideas.

LINKS WITH HOME
Show the parents or carers of dyspraxic childen how to help their children to remember things by using picture lists. For example, a picture of an anorak, a flask, an apple and a backpack could be used to prompt 'getting ready for nursery'.

LEARNING OBJECTIVE FOR ALL THE CHILDREN
● to find out about, and identify, some features of events they observe.

INDIVIDUAL LEARNING TARGET
● to hold, kick, roll a ball, according to their abilities.

Super sport

Group size
Whole group with one adult helper for four to ten children.

What you need
A selection of balls and hoops.

What to do
Introduce this activity by talking about sport and finding out about ball sports together. Plan a whole series of activities in the form of a 'Super sport marathon' or 'Ball bonanza', allowing each child to participate at their own particular level of ability. Have one helper supervise each activity that you choose.

In the series handbook *Special Needs Handbook*, 'differentiation' and 'task analysis' are mentioned. The list below shows the typical steps through which children progress as they learn, develop and perfect various ball skills. This list will help to identify the stage which a child with difficulties has reached, and enable you to plan ways of supporting and encouraging the next steps.

Skills develop in this way:
● Child can hold a small ball with one hand.
● Child learns to hold a large ball with two hands.
● Child can push a ball forward.
● Child can roll a ball in imitation.
● Child can fling a ball to one side, without aim.
● Child can throw a ball into a hoop one metre away.
● Child can throw a ball to an adult one and a half metres away.
● Child can kick a large stationary ball.
● Child can kick a ball when it is rolled to him.
● Child can catch a large foam ball with two hands.
● Child can bounce and catch a large ball.
● Child can run and kick a ball in one movement.
● Child can catch a small foam ball in one hand.

Special support
Plan a child's next step so that, with your support, the child is bound to succeed and therefore to learn.

Extension
Include activities for knocking skittles and dribbling footballs between cones and shooting goals. Talk with the children about why games and sports have 'rules'.

LINKS WITH HOME
When you have decided what step to encourage next, ask parents and carers to practise with their children at home.

LEARNING OBJECTIVES FOR ALL THE CHILDREN
● to find out about the environment
● to find out about living things.

INDIVIDUAL LEARNING TARGETS
● to jump with two feet together
● to jump while carrying a cuddly toy.

LINKS WITH HOME
Tell the child's parents or carers about the success of this bouncing and holding game if you have found it useful for helping their dyspraxic difficulties.

Kangaroo pranks

Group size
Six to ten children.

What you need
A copy of a kangaroo action rhyme such as 'The Kangaroo Song' in *Apusskidu* (A & C Black), or some bouncy music on tape; small cuddly toys.

What to do
This is a very enjoyable activity which children can join in with in a variety of ways. Older and physically able children can bounce to the beat. Other children can bounce in a standing position while being supported, or can be bounced on an adult's knee.

Start by talking about kangaroos and sharing pictures. Consider using the mind-mapping technique (see page 61), representing the keywords visually on a sheet of paper and making associations between them using arrows. This device helps memories and facts to become 'fixed' without the need for the children to remember all the words that went with them.

Follow up by playing some bouncy music or singing a kangaroo action rhyme. The children should sit still for the verse, then bounce in the air for the chorus. Repeat the song two or three times. Introduce small cuddly toys to be 'joeys' and suggest that the children hold them against their tummies as they bounce.

If you feel that the children are getting very excited, try this with a smaller group, or ask them to sit on the floor and pretend that their hands are the kangaroos.

Special support
Bouncing with two feet together while holding a cuddly toy is a particularly helpful exercise for children with dyspraxia. Support children with mobility and balance difficulties at the hands or the hips as they bounce and flex to the rhythm.

Extension
Find some more songs about Noah's ark or zoos to follow the animal theme, such as 'The Animals Went In Two by Two' or 'Going to the Zoo' both in *Apusskidu* (A & C Black). Invent new actions to go with the animals that you chose.

KNOWLEDGE & UNDERSTANDING OF THE WORLD

LEARNING OBJECTIVES FOR ALL THE CHILDREN
● to ask questions about how things work
● to select the tools for a mark-making activity.

INDIVIDUAL LEARNING TARGET
● to practise with a wide range of writing implements.

Pencils and pens

Group size
Three or four children.

What you need
A selection of pencils and washable felt-tipped pens (some chubby and some thinner) to include gold, silver and glitter pens; triangular pencils; selection of pencil and pen grips (see page 96); different shapes, types and colours of paper (see page 96); examples of writing and print from the media; wall area to make a display; large table.

What to do
This activity about pens and pencils involves collecting them, finding out what they do and how, and playing with different styles. It can be used as an extension to 'Getting a grip' on page 44.

Use a large table and spread out the paper and implements. Arrange the materials by colour to make the selection attractive for the children to explore, select and handle. Demonstrate different colour contrasts by making spiky shapes, flowing shapes, thick strokes, thin strokes on different papers.

Gather the children around and have fun experimenting with the different combinations of writing implement and paper. Play with the materials, so that you are enjoying the process as much as the product. Encourage the children to select pieces of mark-making for a gallery display on the wall, mounting them alongside examples of writing and print from the media.

Special support
If a child loses the correct grip, gently use your hand over theirs to re-establish it. Keep this activity particularly motivating and enjoyable if a child has fine-motor difficulties.

Extension
Older children will enjoy writing or copying short pieces of text in different styles and materials.

LINKS WITH HOME
Send home a pack of paper and pens on loan and ask parents and carers to encourage their children to have fun scribbling and mark-making.

SPECIAL NEEDS in the early years: Physical and co-ordination difficulties

PHYSICAL DEVELOPMENT

The activities in this chapter will help all the children to practise moving and balancing with confidence. There are ideas for encouraging postural and movement skills in children who have physical difficulties.

LEARNING OBJECTIVES FOR ALL THE CHILDREN
● to move with confidence, control and safety
● to show awareness of space, of themselves and of others.

INDIVIDUAL LEARNING TARGET
● to creep forward.

Wormy, wormy

Group size
Eight to 20 children.

What you need
A large floor space suitable for creeping and crawling on.

What to do
Encourage the children to remove their shoes and socks and to move into a large space. Help them to hold hands in a circle, and encourage them to spread out until their arms are straight. Then invite them to sit down in a large circle.

Introduce this chant:

> Wormy, wormy, ever so squirmy,
> Wormy, wormy, slippy and wet,
> Wormy, wormy, ever so squirmy,
> Say 'Hello' and home you get!
>
> *Hannah Mortimer*

Now ask the children to lie on their tummies with their heads towards the centre of the circle and to creep forwards very, very slowly as you chant the rhyme. Keep it very steady and slow, and pause on the 'Hello' for everyone to greet each other, then encourage the 'worms' to creep back 'home' to their places again.

Repeat this two or three times, enjoying the eye contact and the greeting as you all come together near the centre. Encourage the children to turn and move safely as they return 'home', and praise them for not bumping into one another.

Special support
Some children with mobility difficulties may still be at the stage of creeping and crawling. Liaise with the physiotherapist and the child's parents or carers about the kinds of movements that you should be encouraging. Use this rhyme to let them to enjoy creeping and crawling along with all the other children.

Extension
Invite the children to think of other ways of moving. Suggest that they think of a frog chant or a kangaroo hop and practise moving accordingly.

LINKS WITH HOME
Adapt this activity as a game at home. Suggest that the parents or carers of the targeted child place favourite toys just out of reach, encouraging their child to creep forward a short distance to claim them.

LEARNING OBJECTIVE FOR ALL THE CHILDREN
● to show awareness of space, of themselves and others.

INDIVIDUAL LEARNING TARGET
● to plan and execute a movement with purpose and co-ordination.

LINKS WITH HOME
Teach the children 'The Scarecrow Song' in *Oranges and Lemons* compiled by Karen King (Oxford University Press) to sing at home.

The scarecrow game

Group size
Six to 20 children.

What you need
A scarecrow's hat, gloves and jacket for yourself; extra helper.

What to do
Wait until the children have all settled well in your group and you feel confident in their responses.

Ask the children to sit on the floor in a circle. Introduce your props and put the items of clothing on. Talk about scarecrows and what they are used for. Now tell the children that you are going to go into the centre of the circle and pretend to be a scarecrow. Ask them to sit still and watch what you do. Tell them they might be surprised!

Move into the centre of the circle and take up a scarecrow stance with your arms out stiffly. Adopt a mournful expression and say, 'I'm a sad scarecrow! I can't move at all!' and then freeze completely.

There may be a moment or two of awkward silence, but then someone is bound to make a move or a noise (or you can prime your helper to do so!). Turn rapidly towards the movement or noise and smile, dancing a little 'jig' for a moment or two. Then freeze again. Very soon, the children will pick up the 'rule' of the drama, and will begin to make noises or movements to which you can respond. Control this by putting on a happy display for a clapping of the hands or a sing-song noise, whatever you choose to 'target'. You can also target certain (shy) children by being particularly delighted and mobile when they give you a vocalization or movement.

Special support
Give a particularly motivating and strong response to whatever movement or vocalization you are targeting for the child with special needs. Ask your helper to sit next to them to suggest, prompt and encourage this if necessary.

Extension
Invite older children to take turns at being the scarecrow.

PHYSICAL DEVELOPMENT • PHYSICAL DEVELOPMENT • PHYSICAL DEVELOPMENT

LEARNING OBJECTIVE FOR ALL THE CHILDREN
● to move with control and co-ordination.

INDIVIDUAL LEARNING TARGET
● to develop balancing skills.

Fishing lines

Group size
Three children.

What you need
A safely-enclosed hard play area outside; chalk; three objects (such as a teddy bear, a car and a ball); the photocopiable sheet on page 92.

What to do
On a dry day set up this activity in advance by chalking three giant fishing lines on the ground (see page 92) as a model for this. The lines should all start from the same end, and then weave loosely in and out of each other until they reach the other side of the play area, about 10 metres away. At the end of each line, place one of the three toys.

Invite three children to play the fishing-line game. Allocate each child one of the lines and point out how the three lines are all muddled up. Ask them where they think their line leads. Invite the children to balance heel to toe along their lines to discover what lies at the end. Encourage them to stay on their lines by balancing carefully. Celebrate their success, re-chalk any lines and invite three more children to join you.

LINKS WITH HOME
Tell parents and carers about this game and that it is ideal to play in the sand on a seaside holiday. Suggest that they bury 'treasure' at the end of each trail!

Special support
For children who are just learning to balance, let them start by walking along straight chalk lines. For children with dyspraxic difficulties, stay by their sides to offer a steadying hand if necessary. For children in wheelchairs, help to push if you need to, while they show you where to go (keep the lines well apart in this case).

Extension
Ask older children to help you set this activity up and chalk the lines.

PHYSICAL DEVELOPMENT · PHYSICAL DEVELOPMENT

LEARNING OBJECTIVE FOR ALL THE CHILDREN
● to move with control and co-ordination.

INDIVIDUAL LEARNING TARGET
● to improve cross-lateral co-ordination.

LINKS WITH HOME
Ask the parents or carers of a dyspraxic child to practise a simple clapping game at home with their child. Explain that they have to face each other with their hands palm forwards, then clap each other's hands as they are, then cross their hands over and clap again as they chant 'Pat-a-cake pat-a-cake, baker's man'.

Cross-overs

Group size
Four to ten children.

What to do
Stand up together, with the children in a line facing you. Choose a simple action and ask the children to copy you. For example, touch your nose repeatedly, then touch the top of your head repeatedly as the children copy.

Next, introduce more complicated movements and ask the children to watch very carefully to see if they can copy you.
● Touch your right knee with your left hand, and then your left knee with your right hand. See if the children can copy, repeating the movements alternately.
● Touch your right ear with your left hand, alternating with the left ear and the right hand.
● Lift and touch your left big toe to your right hand, alternating with the right big toe and the left hand.

Keep the activities fun, sharing the pleasure as you try to increase speed without becoming confused!

Special support
These activities are particularly suitable for children with dyspraxic difficulties. Some people with dyslexia have also reported that this kind of 'brain gymnastics' can improve their ability to scan and decode when they are tried just before a reading or spelling task.

Extension
Challenge older children with more difficult movements, such as 'touch your right knee with your left elbow' and so on. For any dyslexic adults, try crossing your arms as you touch right hand to nose at the same time as left hand to right earlobe, alternating with left hand to nose at the same time as right hand to left earlobe!

LEARNING OBJECTIVE FOR ALL THE CHILDREN
● to move fingers with control and co-ordination.

INDIVIDUAL LEARNING TARGET
● to touch each fingertip to the thumb.

All your fingers

Group size
Four to 12 children.

What you need
A copy of the action song 'Tommy Thumb' in *This Little Puffin...* compiled by Elizabeth Matterson (Puffin Books).

What to do
This is a well-known action rhyme with which the children may already be familiar. Introduce these new actions as part of your usual music-time or circle-time activities.

Hold up one thumb as you sing, 'Tommy Thumb, Tommy Thumb, Where are you?', then wiggle it as you sing 'Here I am, here I am, How do you do?'.

For the next verse, show the children how to oppose their second finger on to their thumb as they sing, 'Peter Pointer, Peter Pointer, Where are you?'. As you add, 'Here I am, here I am, How do you do?', tap your thumb and forefinger together.

In the next verse, hold then tap your middle finger on to your thumb for 'Toby Tall'.

Next comes 'Ruby Ring' for your fourth finger, and finally 'Baby Small' for your little finger.

Sing the rhyme once through for one hand, and then a second time through for the other hand.

Special support
This exercise is helpful for children who have dyspraxic difficulties or who need to improve their fine motor co-ordination. You might need to practise it with the child first, one to one or in a very small group.

Extension
Challenge older children to sing it a third time through, using both hands at the same time!

LINKS WITH HOME
Suggest that the parents or carers of a child with dyspraxia enjoy this action rhyme with their child just before bedtime. At the end, see if their child can oppose each finger to thumb in turn in a quicker movement.

LEARNING OBJECTIVE FOR ALL THE CHILDREN
● to move with confidence and safety.

INDIVIDUAL LEARNING TARGET
● to roll from side to side.

Roly poly

Group size
Two to six children at a time.

What you need
A large floor space; a teddy for each child.

What to do
Ask the children to take off their shoes and socks and to find a space to lie down.
Invite them to lie flat on their backs, looking up at the ceiling, then to lift their arms up and stretch their toes out, making a few gentle stretches as they make themselves as long as possible.
Now introduce this rhyme as the children sit up and watch you:

> Roly poly this way, roly poly back,
> Roly poly this way, roly poly back,
> Roly poly, ever so slowly,
> Touch the floor and back!
>
> *Hannah Mortimer*

For the first two lines, roll gently to one side and then return, and roll to the same side again. Then, on the third line, roll right over to one side, touch the floor and return to your back. Chant a second verse as you repeat the movements to the other side.

Ask each child to help a teddy through the movements as you repeat the rhyme together. Then 'ask' the teddies to watch as the children perform the actions by themselves.

Special support
Some children who are just learning to roll from side to side will enjoy this exercise as an early stage to movement and posture. The physiotherapist might have asked you to rehearse these movements with the child and shown you how. Some children are reluctant to receive direct physiotherapy, and find it much easier to carry out the work when it is made into a rhyme and a game. This activity also allows you to carry out the 'therapy' in an inclusive way among a group of other children.

Extension
Let older children stand up and repeat the rhyme as you reach and stretch down to each side of your bodies as a 'keep fit' exercise!

LINKS WITH HOME
Share the rhyme with the parents or carers of the child that you are targeting in order to make the rolling exercises more fun at home too.

LEARNING OBJECTIVE FOR ALL THE CHILDREN
● to show awareness of space.

INDIVIDUAL LEARNING TARGET
● to move the head with co-ordination when tracking.

Rising sun

Group size
Four to six children.

What you need
A large white sheet; string; torch; means for darkening the room; additional helper; cushions or mat for the children to sit on.

What to do
Tie the sheet in place to make a screen that reaches two metres above the floor, with space behind it for one adult. Place the cushions or mat in front of it, one and a half metres away.

Gather the children together, sitting in front of the screen, and explain that you are going to tell them a story about the sun, and that you need to darken the room for them to be able to see properly.

Darken the windows. As you tell the story, invite the children to follow the 'sun' with their heads, looking at it all the time.

> It is still night-time and all the children are sleeping.
> Look! The sun is peeping over the horizon. It rises slowly into the sky!
> See how it rises and shines now, so that all the children know it is morning time.
> Now the sun is high. It is the middle of the day. The children will eat their lunches.
> The sun begins to go down now. It is afternoon.
> As it sinks down, the children are going to bed.
> Now it is setting. All the children are asleep.

As you tell the story, ask your helper behind the screen to make the torch describe a 180° arc across the sheet, from their right to their left. Finish off by taking turns to make hand shadows behind the screen.

Special support
This will help a child who is learning to make controlled head movements and to track objects and lights. Use any special seating which the child has, to help sitting posture and head control. Stand behind the child and gently support their head as it turns, if the child has difficulty. Praise all their efforts.

Extension
Lead into a shadow puppet story, again encouraging the children to follow the puppets as you tell the story.

LINKS WITH HOME
Show parents and carers how to repeat the exercise with any child that you are targeting by shining a lighted torch on a bedroom wall.

PHYSICAL DEVELOPMENT · PHYSICAL DEVELOPMENT · PHYSICAL DEVELOPMENT

LEARNING OBJECTIVE FOR ALL THE CHILDREN

● to use a range of small equipment.

INDIVIDUAL LEARNING TARGET

● to throw with an approximate aim.

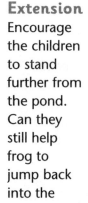

LINKS WITH HOME
Encourage parents and carers to play an aiming game with a beanbag and a waste paper basket at home. See if their children can gradually aim over a longer distance. Ask them to keep this activity fun and successful.

Frogs in the pond

Group size
Eight to 12 children.

What you need
A sheet made of Lycra (3m in diameter); beany frog (or make one out of a beanbag by attaching felt legs and button eyes).

What to do
Stand in a circle (or sit on chairs if one of the children is in a wheelchair) and each hold the edge of the Lycra with two hands. Toss in the frog as you make it gently bounce on the 'pond'. Sing this song to the tune of 'The Farmer's in His Dell' (Traditional):

> Frog's in the pond, frog's in the pond,
> Hip hop hippity hop, frog's in the pond!

Sooner or later, frog is bound to jump out of the pond.

> Frog's jumped out, frog's jumped out,
> Hip hop hippity hop, frog's jumped out!

Invite one of the children to let go of the 'pond' and pick up 'frog'.

> (child's name) has found the frog, (child's name) has found the frog,
> Hip hop hippity hop, (child's name) has found the frog!
>
> *Hannah Mortimer*

Let the child throw frog back into the pond and repeat the verses again until everyone has had a turn at rescuing frog.

Special support
Provide the child that you are targeting with plenty of support as they aim and throw frog back into the pond. Let them stand very close to the pond if they need to.

Extension
Encourage the children to stand further from the pond. Can they still help frog to jump back into the pond?

LEARNING OBJECTIVE FOR ALL THE CHILDREN
- to show awareness of space, of themselves and of others.

INDIVIDUAL LEARNING TARGET
- to change body positions.

LINKS WITH HOME
Provide each child with a copy of the phocopiable sheet on page 93 to enjoy at home. If the child that you are targeting receives physiotherapy including kneeling, prone and lying activities, then this rhyme is ideal for doing your physiotherapy to!

The crocodile song

Group size
12 to 15 children.

What you need
Non-slip footwear for the children.

What to do
Ask the children to remove their shoes and socks and put on plimsolls or rubber-soled slippers. Gather in a circle. Start by standing, but look for ways of including children who cannot stand too (they may need a parent or helper to help them get into different positions). Hold hands and swing arms as you sing the chorus of this song:

> I'm being eaten by a great big crocodile,
> Crunch – slurp – crunch – slurp!
> I'm being eaten by a great big crocodile,
> I don't like it at all!

Now say 'Oh no! He's eaten my toe!' and get on to your knees. Repeat the chorus from your new position, inserting these verses after each chorus:

> Oh my! He's got my thigh!
> *(lie on tummies but push up from the waist)*
> Oh lummy! He's got my tummy!
> *(lie prone with head pushed up)*
> I think I'm dead! He's got my head!
> *(lie flat on tummies)*
> Hurray we shout! He's spat me out!
> *(up you all get)*
>
> *Hannah Mortimer*

Special support
Stay close to any child that you are targeting to help them participate as fully as they can. Allow plenty of time for them to try to move themselves before offering help.

Extension
Look for ways of adapting other traditional circle dances such as 'Here We Go Looby Loo', 'Hokey Cokey', 'In and Out the Dusky Bluebells', 'Wind the Bobbin Up', 'One, Two, Three, Four, Five' to include all the children.

PHYSICAL DEVELOPMENT · PHYSICAL DEVELOPMENT · PHYSICAL DEVELOPMENT ·

LEARNING OBJECTIVE FOR ALL THE CHILDREN
● to move as a group with confidence, imagination, co-operation and safety.

INDIVIDUAL LEARNING TARGET
● to lie and relax.

LINKS WITH HOME
This is a good rhyme for parents to sing with their child with mobility difficulties if they are rocking from side to side and practising 'saving' responses. Some children have to learn how to detect changes in their centre of gravity and put out their hands to steady and 'save' themselves.

Sea-dle-de-dee

Group size
12 to 24 children and two or three additional helpers.

What you need
A parachute (or large sheet cut into an approximate circle); large indoor floor space; rolls of green and blue crêpe paper; cardboard; scissors; pens; silver foil; box.

What to do
Place the craft materials on a table and encourage three or four children at a time to come and help you make the seaweed and fishes for this activity. Cut through strips of crêpe paper in order to make long strands when opened out. Mark the shape of a fish on to card and help each child to cut out a fish, wrap silver foil around it to make it shiny, and use the pens to mark the eyes. Place the fishes on one side in a box.

Gather the children together and kneel in a large circle with the parachute spread out in the middle, so that you are each holding on to the parachute with two hands. Move around the circle, inviting each child in turn to let go of the parachute and choose a fish and some seaweed to toss into the parachute 'sea'. Encourage the children to make gentle wave movements to keep everything in the centre of the parachute, yet stirring with movement.

When everyone has added a fish, introduce this song. The tune is the same as 'Girls and Boys Come Out to Play', shortening the last line to fit.

> Here we are down at the sea-dle-de-dee;
> Waves are as calm as can be-dle-de-dee;
> Fishes can hide in the sea-weed-dle-dee;
> Down at the sea-dle-de-dee!
>
> *Hannah Mortimer*

As you sing, make gentle waves with the parachute.

Special support
Once the sea is under calm control, invite one or two children (including the child that you are targeting) to lie on the floor underneath the 'sea', looking up at the shadows and shapes on the sheet. At another time, you can also include one or two children in the 'sea' by inviting them to lie amongst the seaweed and fishes, rocking them gently to the song. Remove shoes and socks first.

Extension
Ask the children to create more creatures for your parachute sea.

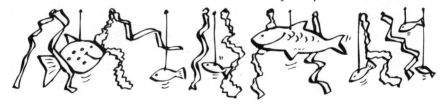

CREATIVE DEVELOPMENT

These activities allow children to play and explore creatively, and include ideas for sensory play and for developing the senses. They have been specially adapted for children who have difficulties with physical co-ordination and mobility.

LEARNING OBJECTIVE FOR ALL THE CHILDREN

● to explore colour, texture and form in two and three dimensions.

INDIVIDUAL LEARNING TARGET

● to move feet with co-ordination and control.

LINKS WITH HOME

Talk to the parents or carers of any child who has a skin condition (such as eczema) to make sure that you are using the right kind of moisturising foam. They may have their own kind which they could lend you. Encourage carers to provide bubble bath at bathtime and to allow their children to enjoy playing with the foam.

Bubble bowl

Group size
Two children.

What you need
A large washing-up bowl; warm water; moisturising bubble bath; children's chairs; towels; plastic sheet.

What to do
Spread the sheet of plastic on the floor and arrange two children's chairs opposite each other on it. Half fill the washing-up bowl with warm water and add plenty of moisturising bubble bath. Place it on a table and ask the children to help mix the bubble bath with their hands until it foams up in peaks. Let them enjoy sculpting the peaks of foam and bubbles, making different shapes. Encourage the children to form shapes on each other's hands. Help them to use gentle blowing to shape the foam.

Now place the bowl on the floor between the two chairs. Encourage the children to take off their shoes and socks, helping where you need to, and to place their feet in the bubbly water. Allow them to make gentle foot movements to sculpt the foam and to pass it from foot to foot. Show them how to use a foot to lift foam carefully on to the sheet and to 'paint' foam pictures on to the sheeting. Admire the foot prints made.

To finish, let the children sit on the chairs and dry each other's feet gently and carefully with the towels.

Special support
This is an ideal activity for a child who is able to enjoy passive play but is not yet able to move their feet and hands with purpose or control. Let the children play with a partner, gently adding and stroking the hands and feet with the foam, enjoying the sights and sensations. For children who are developing sensations in their limbs or learning to control their movements more carefully, this provides an opportunity for developing careful and controlled limb movements and to have fun as well.

Extension
Encourage older children to make a foam sculpture and then draw or photograph it.

LEARNING OBJECTIVE FOR ALL THE CHILDREN
● to respond in a variety of ways to what they see, touch and feel.

INDIVIDUAL LEARNING TARGET
● to make attempts to unwrap a parcel.

LINKS WITH HOME
Suggest that parents and carers make festivals and anniversaries (such as birthdays and Christmas) opportunities for their children to enjoy playing with wrapping paper. Can they help them to wrap and unwrap, selecting the right materials? Ask them to save used wrapping paper for the group to use.

Wrapped up

Group size
Eight to 16 children.

What you need
Plenty of wrapping paper (recycled); sticky tape; selection of soft toys; tape recorder and music; large carton box; 'beautiful object' (such as a decorated egg or a little bell).

What to do
This is a simple version of 'Pass the parcel', with every child being a winner. Wrap up a parcel for each child, placing a soft toy in each one. Some can be wrapped up tightly and stuck with tape, others can be loosely wrapped and therefore easier to unwrap. Put them all in a large carton box.

Ask the children to sit in a circle on the floor. Show them the beautiful object that you have chosen and pass it around the circle, demonstrating which way to pass it, so that each child can have a look at it. Tell the children that when they hear the music playing, they can pass around the object. When the music stops, the child who has the object should keep hold of it. Play 30 seconds or so of music and then stop again. See who is holding the object and pass them a parcel from your box of presents. Encourage them to pass the object to their neighbour and then to unwrap the parcel. Share their surprise as they recognize Hippo or Big Ted. Ask them to place Hippo (or whoever it is!) in front of them and to look after it during the game.

Start the music again and continue until everyone has had a turn. Select 'difficult' parcels for older children, and loosely-wrapped ones for children who might have difficulties opening them. You can see quickly who has not had a turn yet because these will be the children who do not have a soft toy sitting in front of them.

Special support
If a child has difficulties in receiving and passing a small object, choose something large and easy to hold to pass around, such as a large teddy bear. This would also be a useful way to encourage a child to use both hands at once if they tend to ignore one side of their body.

Extension
Older children can help you to set up this activity, choosing the contents of the parcels and wrapping them up.

LEARNING OBJECTIVE FOR ALL THE CHILDREN
● to use their imagination in dance and movement.

INDIVIDUAL LEARNING TARGET
● to hold and wave a scarf.

Rainbow waves

Group size
Eight to 20 children.

What you need
Music on a tape (such as *Bolero* by Ravel); selection of chiffon or light silk scarves in bright colours; instruments such as Indian bells, glockenspiels and chime bars.

What to do
Invite the children to sit on the floor, and throw in the brightly-coloured scarves. Talk about their colours and their textures as you feel them and enjoy their effects. Ask the children what the colours remind them of, and comment on the lovely shapes that they make with the scarves and how they place the bright colours against each other.

Turn the music on softly and encourage the children to enjoy the atmosphere of the waving colours and the waves in the music. Bring out the instruments for the children to explore adding another dimension to their colours and movements. Encourage the children to find their own ways of moving and sound-making as they enjoy the atmosphere that you have created.

Finish by all throwing the scarves lightly in the air and lying down as they flutter and fall around you.

Special support
This is an activity which can be enjoyed passively by a child who has little mobility or co-ordination. You can also use the scarves to encourage the child to hold on to one end as you hold and move the other. Let the child enjoy the soft feel of the fabrics on their hands, their cheeks, even their toes!

Extension
Older children might wish to invent a scarf dance and sound effects to accompany the music.

LINKS WITH HOME
Invite families to help their children to find a beautiful piece of fabric from home to share with the group.

LEARNING OBJECTIVE FOR ALL THE CHILDREN

● to use their imagination in imaginative and role-play.

INDIVIDUAL LEARNING TARGET

● to think of an animal sound and action.

LINKS WITH HOME

Give each child a copy of the photocopiable sheet to take home, talk about and colour in or over. If the child that you are targeting has been asked to practise certain speech sounds at home, such as 'ssss' or 'hu-hu-hu', this rhyme can make the exercise much more fun.

Down in the jungle

Group size
Six to 12 children.

What you need
The photocopiable sheet on page 94.

What to do
Use this activity as part of your regular circle time or music session. Sit on the floor together in a circle and show the children the jungle picture on the photocopiable sheet.

Introduce this rhyme:

> Down in the jungle there's a rumbling sound;
> Something's on the move and it's looking all around.
> Keep very still
> and listen if you will;
> Hide yourself behind a tree and then you won't be found!
>
> *Hannah Mortimer*

Use your tone of voice and gesture to create an atmosphere of quiet listening and anticipation. When everyone is looking and listening, make a tiny sound. It might be the hiss of a snake or the chatter of a little monkey. Ask the children who they think is in the jungle.

Repeat the rhyme as different children take turns to make a jungle sound. Prompt individual children with whispered ideas if they need them.

Special support
Whenever an activity requires the children to sit on the floor in a circle, make sure that this is a position in which any child that you are targeting can sit comfortably and appropriately for their needs. If not, adapt the activity to suit that child. Perhaps they can lie across a wedge while the other children sit on the floor. Perhaps they can sit in their special seat surrounded by the other children on chairs. Make sure that the child is able to join in at the same physical level as the other children.

Extension
Older children might enjoy making jungle pictures which they can show as they make their animal sounds.

LEARNING OBJECTIVE FOR ALL THE CHILDREN
● to use their imagination in art and design.

INDIVIDUAL LEARNING TARGET
● to hold their head steady and look up.

It's only me!

Group size
Three or four children at a time.

What you need
Large cardboard boxes; paints; paintbrushes; plastic sheeting; heavy duty scissors (adult use); full length mirror; camera (optional).

What to do
Explain to the children that they are going to turn a box into a monster or an animal. Let them select a large cardboard box – it might be so big that a child can crouch inside it, or it might just fit over the child's head. Then discuss what kind of monster or animal the children will make. Help them to paint a rough outline of the creature on one side of the box with black paint, making a black blob for the centre of the face (where the children can pop their own faces through later).

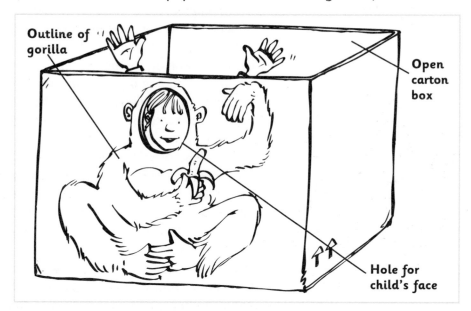

Encourage the children to work together to paint the rest of that side of the box, with bright tiger stripes, colourful dragon blotches or black ape fur. It is more important that the children think of their own ideas and work as a group than that they make a perfect design.

Place the box on one side to dry. Later, cut out the shape of the face. Let the children take turns to place their faces in the space and admire the effects in a mirror. Let the different groups share what they have made with the other children. You could take photographs of the children in the boxes and make a monster display.

Special support
This activity will provide an appropriate moment for encouraging the child with poor neck support to look up and through the hole to see the effect in the mirror.

Extension
Invite the children to use face expressions to add extra effect!

LINKS WITH HOME
Encourage carers and colleagues to use a light chin touch and the child's name to encourage head-raising and eye contact in the child who finds this difficult to do. If necessary, the physiotherapist will be able to show you just how much help to provide and what degree of movement to expect.

LEARNING OBJECTIVE FOR ALL THE CHILDREN
● to explore texture, shape and form in three dimensions.

INDIVIDUAL LEARNING TARGET
● to crumple paper and push it into position.

Sid the snowman

Group size
Three or four children.

What you need
An old white pillowcase; paper; tissues; piece of sheet or muslin; string; black marker pen; hat; scarf; a snowman story and picture book such as *The Snowman* by Raymond Briggs (Hamish Hamilton).

What to do
Wait for a wintry day and talk about building snowmen. Suggest that you build one inside, and when the children challenge you, share your idea with them.

Show the children the materials and suggest that they make the body out of the pillowcase. Show the children how to take pieces of paper or tissue and scrumple these up, stuffing them inside the 'body'. Wrap the muslin cloth around more tissue and draw the edges together with string, attaching it to the bunched top of the pillowcase to make the head.

Follow the children's guidance as you mark with a black pen 'coal' eyes and nose on the head and 'buttons' down the body. Add a hat and a scarf. Encourage other groups of children to join you to help with the scrumpling and filling to make other snowmen.

Finish by reading the children a story about a snowman.

Special support
This activity provides an opportunity for the children to develop the early hand movements involved in tearing, scrumpling and pushing down. Give any child that you are targeting a key role in helping to fill one of the snowmen.

Extension
Encourage older children to make a wintry scene with cotton wool and white crêpe paper for the snowman to stand in.

LINKS WITH HOME
Encourage parents and carers to teach their children to use tissues to wipe their noses and to scrumple and discard them appropriately. Advise them to react positively when the children are successful.

SPECIAL NEEDS **in the early years:** Physical and co-ordination difficulties

LEARNING OBJECTIVE FOR ALL THE CHILDREN
● to respond in a variety of ways to what they see.

INDIVIDUAL LEARNING TARGET
● to raise their head when dorsal.

Shadows on the ceiling

Group size
Three to six children.

What you need
A strong light source (such as an overhead projector); pale wall or ceiling; sheets of coloured acetate (optional); black card; white chalk; scissors; cushions; mats.

What to do
In this game, the children lie on their backs and watch a light shadow display on the ceiling and walls. Experiment with your light source and find a part of the room where you can shine the light up on to a plain wall or ceiling. Arrange the mats and cushions beneath. Place the craft materials on a table nearby.

Invite the children to lie on their backs and watch the lights. Play with different acetates as you enjoy the colours and how they mix together. Use shapes of acetate to produce kaleidoscopic effects. Make your fingers and hands into shapes and shadows such as the head of a rabbit, or the wings of an eagle.

Once your demonstration is over, suggest that the children make shadows and shapes of their own for your light show. Turn the projector off and move to a table. Help the children to chalk an outline on a piece of black paper and cut it out. You might like to follow a theme such as 'Red Riding Hood' or 'Jungle beasts'.

Finish by returning to your light show and telling the story together as you move the children's shapes on the projector plate.

Special support
A physiotherapist or a child's parents or carers will have talked to you about the correct positions and postures to encourage for a child with postural difficulties. Sometimes, one of the exercises that the children have to practise is to raise their heads when lying in a dorsal position. This activity gives the child an enjoyable reason for doing so.

Extension
Older children will be able to put on their own shadow display with your help.

LINKS WITH HOME
Suggest that the carers of a child that you are targeting provide a colourful mobile to encourage their child to lift their head when lying in bed or on a changing mat at home.

CREATIVE DEVELOPMENT · CREATIVE DEVELOPMENT

LEARNING OBJECTIVE FOR ALL THE CHILDREN

● to respond in a variety of ways to what they see, feel and hear.

INDIVIDUAL LEARNING TARGET

● to move their feet.

Lucky legs

Group size
Three to six children.

What you need
A selection of glove puppets; jingly jester hats, jingle bells on ribbons, Indian bells on braid and so on.

What to do
Sit down on the carpet together and take off your shoes. Show the children how you can sit with your feet straight out in front of you and then place the puppets on your feet. Make them dance and bow as the children enjoy your show.

Encourage the children to choose a 'foot puppet' and enjoy an imaginary game together as the puppets communicate and move. Experiment with the jester's hat, placing both feet together inside the hat and making it bob and 'talk' as if it were a head.

Now suggest that such clever feet could also make music. Help the children to attach bells and jingles to their toes and ankles and let them enjoy a foot dance together, still sitting on the carpet.

Special support
This is an activity to encourage purposeful foot movements in a child who is at an early stage of physical development. You might start by lying on an electronic mat (look in your toy catalogue for mats that make sounds as you apply pressure on different parts). Then attach colourful bells or puppets to the toes and encourage the child to make them move, producing a funny effect or sound.

Extension
Make special foot puppets out of old large socks!

LINKS WITH HOME
For children with mobility difficulties, their parents or carers can assemble a noisy mobile in a frame over their children's feet and encourage them to have fun kicking and making musical sounds in a controlled way at home.

CREATIVE DEVELOPMENT · CREATIVE DEVELOPMENT · CREATIVE DEVELOPMENT ·

LEARNING OBJECTIVES FOR ALL THE CHILDREN
● to explore how the sounds of their voices can be changed
● to use their imagination in role-play.

INDIVIDUAL LEARNING TARGET
● to vocalize using repeated vowel sounds.

Monster howls

Group size
Eight to 24 children.

What you need
A large open space with a floor suitable for creeping along.

What to do
Ask the children to hold hands in a large circle and to step back until their arms are straight. Now ask them to let go of each other's hands and sit down.

Challenge the children to think of a sound that would come out of a friendly monster's mouth. Share a few ideas and practise the sounds. You might choose a repeated vowel sound, such as 'oo-oo-oo-oo', or a two-syllable chatter, for example, 'oo-ah-oo-ah', or even a gentle growl such as 'grrrrrr'.

Ask the children to lie on their tummies with their heads towards the centre of the circle. Say that the monsters are going to come into the centre to say 'Hello' to one another. Creep slowly in as you repeat the monster sound, raising your voices as you approach the centre. Now gradually straighten up to a standing position, raising your hands high and increasing the volume. Lower your hands, crouch down again and creep safely back, slowly quietening your voices as you leave one another.

Keep this fun by friendly eye contact and smiling, and allow the children to watch at first if they prefer to. Encourage eye contact as the 'monsters' greet one another in the centre.

LINKS WITH HOME
Ask parents and carers to keep you in touch with the targets that the speech and language therapist, occupational therapist or physiotherapist have set for the child that you are working with. Consider using a three-way therapist–home–setting diary.

Special support
Use this activity for the child that you are targeting to practise lying on their front, creeping and crawling, standing and repeating speech sounds, depending on the particular target for that child. You could choose sounds that the child is practising at that time, for example, blowing sounds such as 'hu-hu-hu', or hard consonants such as 'k-k-k-k'. For a child who has difficulties with speech expression, the speech and language therapist might have asked you to focus on certain speech sounds.

Extension
Extend this activity into a monster dance and encourage the children to invent movements and sounds to accompany it.

LEARNING OBJECTIVE FOR ALL THE CHILDREN
● to express and communicate their ideas by using a widening range of materials and role-play.

INDIVIDUAL LEARNING TARGET
● to move their bodies with developing control.

Rattlesnakes

Group size
Six to ten children.

What you need
An indoor carpeted floor space (not too large); newspapers; crinkly wrapping paper; shakers; rattles.

What to do
Prepare this activity by tossing crumpled newspaper and crinkly wrapping paper all over the floor area. Tell the children that you are going to play a hiding game together, and ask each child to choose a rattle or a shaker.

Have fun as you encourage the children to creep underneath the paper with their rattles and shakers and to hide. Check if they are completely hidden. Can they see you? Can you see them? Make a game of pretending that you have no idea where a child is and invite the child to shake their rattle and see if you can lift the right piece of newspaper to find them underneath.

Invite a child to be your helper. Ask the hidden children by name to take it in turns to shake their rattles. Then ask your helper to point to where the 'rattlesnakes' are, so that you can gently step in and uncover them. Encourage the other 'snakes' to lie very still so that they do not make a noise.

Special support
This allows a child with mobility difficulties to join in fully. It can be used to encourage lying and hand control. Because you are doing the uncovering, there should be no danger of the hidden snakes being stepped on!

Extension
Make rattlesnakes out of cotton reels and large beads threaded on to bootlaces. Place dry pasta shapes in an empty plastic spice container. Make a small hole in the lid and thread the tail end of the bootlace through. This will make a rattly tail to go on the end of your snake!

LINKS WITH HOME
Show parents and carers how to adapt this activity as a 'Hide-and-seek' activity at home.

Individual education plan

Name:	Early Years Action/Action Plus:

Nature of difficulty:

Action	Who will do what?
1. Seeking further information	
2. Seeking training or support	
3. Observations and assessments	
4. Encouraging learning and development	

What exactly do we wish to teach and encourage?

How will we do this?

What opportunities will we make for helping the child to generalize and practise these skills throughout the session?

How will we make sure that the child is fully included in the early years curriculum?

Help from parents or carers:

Targets for this term:

How will we measure whether we have achieved these?

Review meeting with parents or carers:

Who else to invite:

Hungry clown

Memories

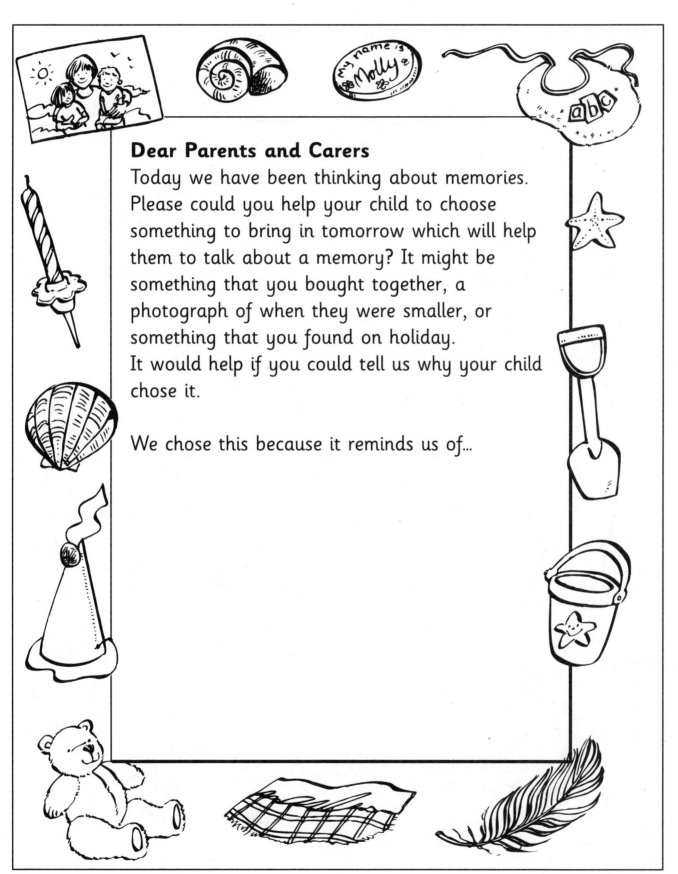

Dear Parents and Carers

Today we have been thinking about memories. Please could you help your child to choose something to bring in tomorrow which will help them to talk about a memory? It might be something that you bought together, a photograph of when they were smaller, or something that you found on holiday.

It would help if you could tell us why your child chose it.

We chose this because it reminds us of...

Journey to the bottom of the sea

Today we enjoyed a sound story about a journey under the sea. Ask your child to tell you about this picture.

Story felts

Wheels

How many wheels can you see?

   SPECIAL NEEDS **in the early years:** Physical and co-ordination difficulties

At home

Who lives where? Can you draw a line to show each creature the way home?

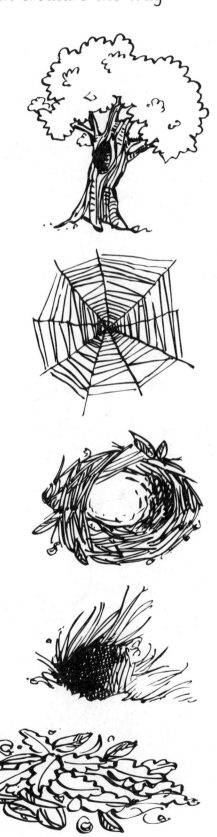

Fishing lines

Can you trace these lines with your finger? Who has caught the fish?

 SPECIAL NEEDS **in the early years:** Physical and co-ordination difficulties

The crocodile song

I'm being eaten by a great big crocodile,
Crunch – slurp – crunch – slurp!
I'm being eaten by a great big crocodile,
I don't like it at all!

Oh no! He's eaten my toe!
Oh my! He's got my thigh!
Oh lummy! He's got my tummy!
I think I'm dead! He's got my head!
Hurray we shout! He's spat me out!

Hannah Mortimer

Down in the jungle

SPECIAL NEEDS in the early years: Physical and co-ordination difficulties

RECOMMENDED RESOURCES

ORGANIZATIONS AND SUPPORT GROUPS

● Association for Spina Bifida and Hydrocephalus, ASBAH House, 42 Park Road, Peterborough, PE1 2UQ. Tel: 01733-555988.

● The British Association of Occupational Therapists, 106–114 Borough High Street, Southwark, London SE1 1LB. Tel: 020-73576480.

● The *CaF Directory* of specific conditions and rare syndromes in children with their family support networks can be obtained on subscription from Contact a Family, 209–211 City Road, London EC1V 1JN. Tel: 020-76088700.

● Chartered Society of Physiotherapy, 14 Bedford Row, London WC1R 4ED. Tel: 020-73066666.

● The Dyspraxia Foundation, 8 West Alley, Hitchin, Herts SG5 1EG. Tel: 01462 454986. Contact them for a list of useful publications.

● SCOPE, 6 Market Road, London N7 9PW. Cerebral Palsy Helpline: 0808-8003333.

BOOKS FOR ADULTS AND FOR CHILDREN

● *All Together: How to Create Inclusive Services for Disabled Children and Their Families* by Mary Dickins and Judy Denziloe (National Early Years Network)

● *Inclusion in Pre-school Settings: Support for Children with Special Needs and Their Families* by Chinelo Chizea, Ann Henderson and Gabriel Jones can be obtained from the Pre-school Learning Alliance (address on page 96).

● *Special Needs and Early Years Provision* by Hannah Mortimer (Continuum)

● *More Quality Circle Time* by Jenny Mosley (Learning Development Aids). Contains ideas on using circle time in nursery and Reception, including the use of puppets, drama and guided imagery.

● *Understanding Developmental Dyspraxia* by Madeleine Portwood (David Fulton)

● *Dyspraxia: A Guide for Teachers and Parents* by Kate Ripley, Bob Daines and Jenny Barrett (David Fulton)

● *What Works in Inclusive Education?* by Judy Sebba and Darshan Sachdev (Barnardo's)

● *Tibby Tried It* by Sharon and Ernie Useman. It is a picture book for young children about coping with physical disability. Tibby is a bird with a crooked wing who will never be able to fly. Available through Magination Press (address below).

● Magination Press, c/o The Eurospan Group, 3 Henrietta Street, Covent Garden, London WC2E 8LU. Tel: 020-72400856. Books that help children to deal with a variety of personal problems.

WEBSITES

● The Department for Education and Skills (DfES) (for parent information and for Government circulars and advice, including the *SEN Code of Practice*): www.dfes.gov.uk

● Tumble Tots and Gymbobs (to find out about local classes): www.tumbletots.com

● The Writers' Press, USA, publish a number of books for young children about a range of SEN: www.writerspress.com

EQUIPMENT SUPPLIERS

- Anything Left-handed Ltd, 57 Brewer Street, London, W1R 3FB. Tel: 020-74373910. Resources and equipment for left-handers.
- Philip Green Education, from Hope Education, Hyde Buildings, Ashton Road, Hyde, Cheshire SK14 4SH. Tel: 0870-2433400. For colourful poster packs.
- KCS, FREEPOST, Southampton SO17 1YA. Specialist tools for making computer equipment accessible to all children.
- Learning Development Aids (LDA), Duke Street, Wisbech, Cambridgeshire PE13 2AE. Tel: 01945-463441. Supply the *Circle Time Kit* by Jenny Mosley, which contains puppets, rainstick, magician's cloak and many props for making circle time motivating. Also supply *Write From the Start*, which offers a unique approach to handwriting.
- National Association of Toy and Leisure Libraries, 68 Churchway, London NW1 1LT. Send sae to find out where the nearest toy library is.
- NES Arnold, Findel House, Excelsior Road, Ashby Park, Ashby-de-la-Zouch, Leicestershire LE65 1NG. Tel: 0870-6000192.
- The Paper Mill Shop, Burneside Mills, Kendal, Cumbria LA9 6PZ. Tel: 01539-818484. (Or McArthurGlen Designer Outlets, St Nicholas Avenue, Fulford, York YO19 4TA. Tel: 01904-674822.) Supply affordable coloured paper and card in a range of colours and textures.
- *Playsense: A Guide and Resource for Play for Babies and Young Children* by Charles Barnard and Sabina Melidis. This pack of play cards to help younger children is available from Play Matters through the National Association of Toy and Leisure Libraries (address above).

- Step by Step, Lee Fold, Hyde, Cheshire SK14 4LL. Tel: 0161-3672800. Supply toys for all special needs, including two-handed scissors and pencil grips.

ORGANIZATIONS THAT PROVIDE TRAINING COURSES

- Children in Scotland, Princes House, 5 Shandwick Place, Edinburgh EH2 4RG. Tel: 0131-2288484. Courses in early years, including SEN.
- Makaton Vocabulary Development Project, 31 Firwood Drive, Camberley, Surrey GU15 3QD. Tel: 01276-671368. Information about Makaton sign vocabulary and training.
- National Association for Special Educational Needs (NASEN), 4–5 Amber Business Village, Amber Close, Amington, Tamworth, Staffordshire B77 4RP. Tel: 01827-311500. For publications and workshops on all aspects of SEN.
- National Children's Bureau, 8 Wakley Street, London EC1V 7QE. Tel: 020-78436000. Many seminars and workshops on children and SEN.
- National Early Years Network, 77 Holloway Road, London N7 8JZ. Tel: 020-76079573. For customized in-house training.
- Pre-school Learning Alliance National Centre, 69 Kings Cross Road, London WC1X 9LL. Tel: 020-78330991. Information on DPP courses and their special needs certificate. Free catalogue, order form and price list of publications available).
- Many voluntary organizations (such as SCOPE) run training courses. Contact them for details.